BOSTON COMMON

A DIARY OF NOTABLE EVENTS, INCIDENTS, AND NEIGHBORING OCCURRENCES

By SAMUEL BARBER

"Author of "Trash; a Society Novel", "A Matrimonial Experiment," Etc.

CHRISTOPHER PUBLISHING HOUSE

BOSTON

Marula

An imprint of Arcadia Publishing

A View of Boston Common
A Diary of Notable Events, Incidents, and Neighboring Occurrences
by Samuel Barber

A Marula Historical Reprint
Originally published in 1914

Published by Arcadia Publishing
Charleston SC

ISBN 978-0-7385-9490-3

Printed in the United States of America

For all general information contact Arcadia Publishing at:
Telephone 843-853-2070
Fax 843-853-0044
E-mail sales@arcadiapublishing.com
For customer service and orders:
Toll-Free 1-888-313-2665

Visit us on the Internet at www.arcadiapublishing.com

THE CHRISTOPHER PRESS
BOSTON, U. S. A.

To

Miss Lois Hildegarde Hall

of New York

With the warmest friendship I inscribe this volume

FOREWORD

Boston Common belongs to the world. In or around it took place events which link it with the history of government for and by the people in this country. From it radiated the influences that led to democratic as opposed to aristocratic rule. To it can be traced the gatherings in town halls by the substantial men in Massachusetts, and other commonwealths; and the famous little red schoolhouses date their inspiration from the public exercises that took place on the classic green in Boston. As the years have progressed, interest in the Boston Common has increased year by year. Details that appeared to be of slight moment in the early history of the country are now sought after. Whatever has taken place there or in the vicinity of it has become in a sense hallowed to the lover of liberty.

The very great distance in time between the present and the early planting of Boston Common, together with the apparent neglect of chroniclers of events in connection with it, has made difficult the collation of facts respecting the time honored centre of Boston. The author has endeavored to faithfully and chronologically register the results of his researches in the following pages. Accuracy has been his one desire and care. It is that feature on which he bases his right to be heard, and on which he believes that his efforts will be of profit to the reader. To those who have aided him, either by advice or by their registered dates, he returns his thanks and acknowledgements.

BOSTON.

Boston, the American Athens, stands in the front rank of social, commercial and political prominence. The reputation of families of culture has spread throughout the country, and its leading men, as one generation has followed another, have wielded a mighty influence in moulding public opinion and promoting its resources. It abounds in historic landmarks, which date from Colonial days, and its modern development, with its broad avenues, buildings and parks, has equalled, if not excelled, any city in the world.

THE COMMON.

The Common, with all its historic associations, is now the Park of the City with its fountains, statues, malls and lake. It has always been the scene of all kinds of incidents—historic, dramatic, tragic, and is now the feature in its landscape and beauty. It might be called an indicator of all that ever occurred in Boston.

COLONIAL PERIOD

1623

Three years after the "Landing of the Pilgrims" a number of patents were granted by the Council of New England, one being granted to William Blackstone at Shawmut (the Indian name meaning glistening fountain), on the Peninsula. Blackstone (called by some Blaxton) and known as "Boston's First Inhabitant" lived on his farm comprising eight hundred acres. He was a graduate of an English University and entering the ministry, was ordained in the church where, unable to conform to the strict laws and desiring "to get from under the power of the lords-bishops" came to America. He lived alone and, known as the "Hermit of Shawmut," enjoyed a tranquil repose. The locality of his house, a slight frame structure, is a matter of much doubt. Savage, Shaw, Snow, Drake, Shurtleff, Howe and others, variously place it on the westerly part of the Peninsula near the present Louisburg Square, Blackstone's Point, on Cambridge Bay, Barton's Point, Poplar or Cambridge Street, the vicinity of Charlestown Bridge and on the southwest slope of Beacon Hill with Cotton and Vane for neighbors, and also bounded by Beacon, Spruce and Pinckney Streets and the Charles River.

A patent was granted, by the Council of New England to Winthrop who, with his colony, now held all its rights with that of Massachusetts which lay outside of Plymouth and extended to the Atlantic Ocean.

John Lothrop Motley in the charming novel "Merry Mount" (1849), "A Romance of the Massachusetts Colony," says—"It was in a secluded cove, with the bay in front, the three headed hill of Shawmut in the distance, and the primeval forest stretching out, in unfathomable shade, behind and all around.

The cottage was simple and rude, but picturesque in its effects. It was built of logs, which still retained their dark and mossy bark. It covered a considerable extent of ground; the thatched roof was low browed, with steep gables at the end, and two or three were furnished with small diamond panes of glass, a luxury which was at that day by no means common even in England. Over the door, which opened on the outside with a wooden latch, stood a pair of moose antlers, and on the ends of the projecting rafters, under the eaves, were suspended the feet of wolves, the tails of foxes, raccoons, and panthers, and other trophies of the chase. On the sward of Wildgrass around the house lay a heap of wild game which had recently been thrown there,—pied brant-geese, blue and green winged teal, two or three long necked, long-billed cranes, with a rabblerout of plump slate colored pigeons, lay promiscuously with a striped bass, dappled sea trout and other fish. It was evident that, although the sporting season had nearly reached its termination, there was yet no danger of starvation."

Hawthorne, in "Twice Told Tales," says in the chapter entitled "The May Pole of Merry Mount,"—

"Bright were the days at Merry Mount, when the May Pole was the banner staff of that gay Colony! They who reared it, should their banner be triumphant, were to pour sunshine over New England's rugged hills, and scatter flower seeds throughout the soil. Jollity and gloom were contending for empire. Midsummer eve had come, bringing deep verdure to the forest, and roses in her lap, of a more vivid hue than the tender buds of Spring. But May, or her mirthful spirit, dwelt all the year round at Merry Mount, sporting with the summer months, and revelling with Autumn, and basking in the glow of Winter's fireside. Through a world of toil and care she flitted with a dream like smile, and came hither to find a home among the lightsome hearts of Merry Mount."

1630

Dr. Holmes, in a poetical description, says:

"Beneath the shaggy southern hill
Lies wet and low the Shawmut plain.
And hark! the trodden branches crack;
A crow flaps off with startled scream;
A straying woodchuck canters back;
A bittern rises from the stream;
Leaps from his lair a brightened deer;
An otter plunges in the pool;
Here comes old Shawmut's pioneer,
The parson on his brindled bull."

SUMMER.

The Arbella came, with other vessels, bringing the Winthrop Colony, which, after enduring many hardships arising from impure water, hunger, exposure, and disease, settled at Charlestown. Blackstone, touched by their suffering, asked the Colony to cross the river and share his grounds, which, with other advantages, abounded in pure springs, shade, trees and pasture and relinquished to their use nearly all of his land, keeping only fifty acres and his own house which had covered his head for several years. His philanthropy extended and in a few years "finding that he had fallen under the power of the lords brethren" he also donated to the Colony the remainder of his estate, retaining but six acres for his own use, for which he was paid six shillings from each householder, though, in some instances, larger sums were paid *pro rata*—for the release. The sum aggregated about £30, which was mainly owing to the efforts of Governor Winthrop who was foremost in many public movements, Blackstone only claiming the honor of being the first discoverer and pioneer. The grounds now surrendered were appropriated as a "Common and Training Field." They extended as far as the present Tremont Building and bounded by the present Beacon, Spruce and Pinckney Streets and the Charles River.

Among the early settlers of Boston were John Odlin, Robert Walker,—the first who had settled on the Peninsula of Boston,—Francis Hudson, and William Lytherland "ancient dwellers" and inhabitants of the town of Boston, who purchased from William Blackstone "his estate and right in any lands lying within said Neck called Boston," for which every housekeeper was taxed six shillings, "some less, some considerably more." Upon this purchase the town laid out the "Common," as a "Training Field" and for the feeding of cattle to be known as common land and common to all the inhabitants.

Two large trees that once stood on the Common have become a part of American history;—the "Liberty Tree" and the "Old Elm." The "Liberty Tree" was in a grove of elms at the corner of Essex and Washington Streets, opposite the Boylston Market, and, like the "Charter Oak" at Hartford, was destined to figure prominently in the early Colony.

The famous "Old Elm," stood near the centre of the Common, and, it is said, was growing when discovered by the first settlers. Two other trees are said to have then stood, probably toward Park Street. These four trees were all that were then on the Common. Winthrop may have enjoyed the shade of the "Old Elm" when he was asked by Blackstone to cross over from Charlestown, in August, to explore the locality for a new settlement, perchance, John Wilson may have preached his first sermon upon the Peninsula, and that the ancestral tribes of Obbatinewat and Squaw Sachem danced to many a Savage Feast around the Indian fire where the kettle hung suspended from three cross poles in the centre of the round group. Some authorities say it was never known who planted the "Old Elm," again, it is said to have been transplanted by Hezekiah Henchman, —when a boy—and an uncle of Governor Hancock, from the North end, about 1670, or his father—Daniel —at an earlier period. Rings counted in the "Old Elm," in 1860, showed it to have grown as early as 1630. When the time came that fears were felt for the "Old Monarch," an iron clamp held one of its large limbs to the trunk, but which broke its bondage by its weight. Another limb was held by a rope while a round iron fence prevented injury by pedestrians walking on the Common which was then, alternately, designated as "Centry," "Century," and "Training Field."

1632 MAY 24.

The people of Charlestown, Roxbury and Dorchester began to build a Fort at the top of Beacon Hill.

Beacon Hill resembled a sugar loaf.

1634

A garden stood on the west side of Beacon Hill.

Century, afterwards called Beacon Hill, on the Common.

1635

Beacon Hill, known in Colonial days as Tri-mountain and afterwards as Sentry Hill, got its last name when (1635) the Beacon was erected on its top by order of the General Court of the Colony, and which, as an alarm signal, made it a spot of great interest. It was the first point of land seen when the early settlers approached the shores of Massachusetts and the place where they landed after entering the harbor—the Beacon, with three peaks, showed the lantern, hung from a tall pole, resting on cross timbers with a stone foundation, with iron crane and hook, projecting from one side, intended to alarm the inhabitants in the event of an attack by the Indians. The Beacon was gradually ascended from the south and southeast sides, and now though reduced in height and covered by buildings, it is still the highest point of land on the Peninsula though it cannot be seen from any distance in the city. The State House, in its stately grandeur, occupies the top and the glistening golden dome exceeds the early heighth of the hill which the colonists and townspeople climbed and looked afar off on the broad expense of meadow and ocean. Its first name—Tre-mount—came by its three hills. It had no name when Blackstone occupied the Peninsula, and its present name when it became the "lookout" of the town and weekly drills were held on the "Training Field," though its "Central" position, the building of the "Fort" (1632) and the "Windmill" gave it temporary designation. The settlement was, at different times, known as Shawmut, Tra-M[illegible]ntaine and Boston and prior to that, Blackstone's Neck. One of the three small hills, which formed the group, was named "Cotton Hill" that stood near the end of Pemberton Square, nearly opposite to King's Chapel Burying Ground. Rev. John Cotton, (for whom it was named) lived near the hill on what is now Tremont Row. It was afterward called Pemberton Hill. One of the Mathers says that three hundred skulls supposed to be those of Indians, were dug up on Cotton Hill, showing a once Indian population on the Peninsula, yet no other evidences were found in any of the many excavations in early Boston. Beacon Hill, seen from Charlestown, was flat for a small space on the top where the "Light" was seen. It was a pasture for cattle and abounded in barberry and wild rose bushes. The march of improvements has entirely changed two of the hills, but it has often been regretted that the entire group could not have been preserved for their historic associations. The Common saved Beacon Hill, now marked by a monument.

Shawmut, the original name of the Peninsula, signifies "living fountains."

The Beacon Light was erected on Centry Hill.

1637 MAY 13.

The First Pound was established soon after the opening of the Common. The first record of the "fould keeper" bears the above date.

SEPTEMBER 28.

William S. Schouler was hanged, on the Common, for murder.

1638 JUNE 1.

A severe earthquake occurred in Boston and was felt on the Common.

JUNE 5.

The journal of Governor Winthrop alludes to the arrival of ships with a respectable class of people aboard and, although no names of either ships or passengers are mentioned, yet, doubtless, John Josselyn, Gentlemen, a scientific scholar, came in one of them. He crossed in a vessel called the New Supply, alias, the Nicholas, of London; Robert Taylor, Master, with one hundred and sixty-four passengers including men, women and children. Several died during the voyage from small-pox and other diseases. The Nicholas, arriving in the port of Boston came to anchor in the inner bay. Mr. Josselyn became the guest (July 10th) of Mr. Maverick, on Noddles Island, whom he says was "the only hospitable man in all the country, giving entertainments to all comers gratis." In describing his visit to Boston, he also says: "Having refreshed myself for a day or two, upon Noddles Island I crossed the bay in a small boat to Boston which then was rather a village than a town there being not above twenty or thirty houses. And presenting my respects to Mr. Winthrop, the Governor, and to Mr. Cotton, the Teacher, of Boston Church to whom I delivered, from Mr. Francis Quarles, the poet, the translation of the Psalms into English meter, for his approbation; being civilly treated by all I had occasion to converse with. I returned in the evening to my lodgings." John Josselyn, probably came over to visit his brother who was living at Black Point, and—July 20—sailed for the eastern coast. His visit was made up of rambles about the country in which he found both amusement and admiration. He climbed steep declivities with his gun hung on his back, shot wolves that had been killing goats and killed snakes some being three yards long. He returned to Boston, September 24th, after a three days sail and visited a ship of 500 tons—Mr. Henderson; Master, lying in the harbour, also a privateer, the—Queen of Bohemia—Captain Jackson, and, landing in the town, procured some refreshments at the "Ordinary" (Inn). The next morning he was invited to a fisherman's house, in the bay, where the fisherman's wife presented him with a "handful of small pearl, but none of them bored, nor Orient." He visited Charlestown where, in "Long's Ordinary," he met Captain Jackson, and made other acquaintances, when all took a walk encountering a rattlesnake long enough to swallow a live chicken. He visited a ship, during the afternoon, when he had the sight of an Indian pinnacle, sailing by—made of birch bark, sewed together with roots of spruce and white cedar (drawn out into threads) with a deck and trimmed with sails, top and top-gallant, very sumptuously." He returned to the house of Mr. Maverick, on Noddles Island—September 30, where having been three months lacking a week—since July 3rd—he remained until he sailed for England. Rambling through the woods "on the back side of the house," during the short interval prior to his departure, one day he saw a wasp's nest which he thought was "a fruit like a pineapple" notwithstanding, "it was planted with scales and as big as the crown of a woman's hat," and attempting to gather it caused a swarm of wasps to fly around his head one stinging him on the upper lip which so disfigured his face that he became unrecognizable and was only known by the clothes he wore. On his departure, the ship laid at Nantasket for some days before proceeding to sea, when the Master, Captain Luxon, came ashore, on Governor's Island, returning with some pippins of which he gave ten to Mr. Josselyn, who said, "there is not an apple tree, nor pear tree, yet planted, in no part of the country, but upon that Island."

Dorothy Talbe, an insane woman, who had killed her child to save it from future punishment, was hanged, probably, on the Common. It was believed that the deed had been prompted by the devil who would be justly retributed by her death.

1640 MARCH 30.

A man was chosen to "keep the cowes which goe on the Common," who was paid "two shillings and sixpence the head for every cowe that goes there." A few years afterward a shepherd was appointed.

A law was passed for the protection of the Common. It was provided that "no land should be sold for either house plot or garden between Sentry Hill and Mr.

Colbron's end save three or four lots required for a street from Brother Robert Walker's to the Round Marsh. Edward Bayties, being at Isle Sables, shall have six months to build on his lot. Ordered that the street from Mr. Atherton Haughe's to Sentry Hill be laid out and kept open for ever. William Davis, gunsmith, to have 20 acres at the Mount. William Briscoe, tailor, to have lot between Robert Walker's and the Round Marsh and to look to the fences, Richard Fairbanks and William Salter, the field toward Roxbury; Benjamin Gillam and Edward Jacklyn the Fort field, William Hudson and Edward Bendall the New field; Mr. Valentine Hill and John Button, the Millfield." To prevent any further encroachments three commissioners were sent to England.

1641

The new slope of the Centinel Hill was familarly called "Zachariah Phillips five acre pasture."

1643 MARCH 21.

James Britton and Mary Latham were hanged on the Common for murder.

Boston was visited by a distinguished Frenchman—La Tour—who, having had invalided claims, bequeathed by his father, in Nova Scotia, thought himself entitled to consideration by the English colonists. A rivalry in trade had broken out between La Tour and D'Aulney who had a trading post on the Penobscot and had become Governor of Arcadie. The case was carried to the French Courts and La Tour was given possession of the Fort, and the right to establish a house at the mouth of the St. Johns and the entire Arcadian peninsula except

—Port Royal and Le Havre, La Tour, having broken up the trading house between Plymouth and Machias, May 4th, and defying the King, entered Boston harbor in a ship full of armed men and first sent word in a shallop to Governor Winthrop who, with his family, were residing on an island. The sight of the vessel created great alarm among the inhabitants who rushed to arms. The Governor was advised to come to Boston! Three shallops were rowed ashore, La Tour in one of them, who, presenting his commission, asked leave to land his men, saying that he had sailed away from Rochelle and, unable to enter the harbor of St. Johns, blockaded by D'Aulney with two ships and five hundred men, had sailed for Boston, also saying he would land them in small companies to prevent any excitement. Permission was granted and a "training day" set when Governor Winthrop dined the officers at his house and the town soldiers welcomed the men to their homes. Forty soldiers, in full uniform, led by Rev. John Cotton and the colonial train land—numbering one hundred and fifty were then escorted to the Common, where they were drilled in the presence of the Governor, a number of Magistrates and a large concourse of people who thought them to be very expert in their manoeuvres, but the "sudden attack" so frightened the women and children that it was declared to be highly imprudent to have allowed them to leave the vessel. La Tour became well acquainted with a number of Boston merchants and, with an air of great piety, attended meetings and lectures. He obtained the consent of Winthrop to charter vessels and hire men for the relief of St. Johns, and, with a fleet of four ships besides his own, proceeded there, breaking the blockade and compelling D'Aulney to flee to Port Royal. Governor Winthrop's action made him very unpopular. La Tour returned to Boston (1645) soliciting and, but only received deep reprobation and then went to New Foundland and again shortly afterward, returned to Boston living for a winter on the charity of friends, his sailors wandering in great distress about the streets.

1644 APRIL 8.

William Franklin was hung on the Common for murder.

APRIL 9.

Gallows were erected on the Common.

AUGUST 26.

A large meteor caused great consternation on the Common.

During the Civil War in England a war vessel, commanded by Captain Stagg, arrived at Boston without exchanging signals with the Beacon. Encountering a Bristol ship, in the harbor, in sight of the Common, it compelled it to surrender much to the surprise of the inhabitants, who wondered how any such liberty could be taken without a commission from the Earl of Warwick. As the City of Bristol had surrendered to the Royalists, a year before, all her ships were claimed as prizes to the ships of Parliament. No interference was attempted, but the Colonists passed a law "not to permit any ship to fight in the harbor without license from authority," thus ignoring any Parliamentary Commission from that time.

1646 May 18.

A proclamation of Governor Winthrop restricted the Common to the exclusive use of the inhabitants of the town. No person could dispose of the privilege and no dry cattle, young cattle, or horse should be permitted there, and that only seventy cows and Elder Oliver's horse should graze, under the penalty of a fine. One cow only could be grazed by one person, which law was altered a few years afterward allowing four sheep instead of a cow, if desired. The keeper's fee was two shillings and sixpence for each cow, eight pence for a sheep and three pence for a lamb.

Boston had another distinguished visitor in Captain Cromwell, the Buccaneer, in command of three brigantines armed with cannon and a full number of men. Cromwell carried a kind of commission from the Earl of Warwick by which he claimed authority to act on the sea, and proceeding to the West Indies captured three Spanish prizes each with a valuable cargo. Encountering a storm his little fleet were driven into Plymouth which Winthrop thought to be an act of divine providence "so directing for the comfort and help of the town which was now almost deserted." The visitors spent their money freely and gave liberally to the poor, yet were watched closely by the Plymouth magistrates by virtue of their authority. Cromwell and his men came to Boston where, it was said, "he and all his men had much money and great stores of plate and jewels of great value, yet, he took up his lodging in a poor, thatched house; and, when he was offered the best in the town, his answer was, that "in his mean estate that poor man entertained him when others would not, and therefore he would not leave him now, when he might do him good." He presented Winthrop with an elegant Sedan chair found among his prizes and was thought to have been intended by the Viceroy of Mexico as a gift to his sister. Captain Cromwell also members of his crew were seen on the Common.

1647 MARCH 29.

Digging sods was forbidden on the Common.

1648 JUNE 15.

Witchcraft in New England recalls an exciting period when suspected persons were thought to be in direct communication with the evil one, and, who, under his direct influence, worked different forms of iniquity to their neighbors, and, regarded as cruel, revengeful and bloody, became a pest to society. Almost every domestic mishap was supposed to have been caused by some "bewitched" person, who, being tried, was in some instances, put to death. The first execution for witchcraft in Boston on this date was that of Margaret Jones, the wife of Thomas Jones of Charlestown who, also, was arrested and tried on the same charge, but was acquitted. She was a doctress who used simple remedies composed of anise seed, liquors, etc., but, which, administered in small doses, produced wonderful effects. Probably her words were a source of healing through the mind, while her touch was said to impart a charm. She had bewitched no one, but was arrested on the charge of possessing imps. Her trial created much excitement as the General Court was composed of Governor Winthrop, who presided, and was assisted by Thomas Dudley, Deputy Governor John Endicott, Richard Bellingham, Richard Saltonstall, Increase Nowell, Simon Bradstreet, William Hibbins (whose widow was executed for witchcraft) John Winthrop, Jr., and William Pynchon (who afterward presided over the examinations at Springfield) all of whom were founders of the Colony. Margaret Jones was convicted on six charges, four were: (1) that her malignant touch on many persons, under any circumstances produced deafness, vomiting, violent pains, etc. (2) The violent effects that resulted from her simple medicines. (3) That she declared cure to be hopeless to all who refused to take her medicines causing them to relapse into a worse condition. (4) That she prophesied events that came to pass and of which, it was thought, she had no knowledge.

During her trial she falsified and insulted the Court and witnesses by loud imprecations. The Court and Deputy's records mention no names, but say that the Court will pursue the same method as that followed in England to watch and discover witches and, alluding to Margaret Jones, orders that she be watched each night, and, also her husband who was confined in a separate room. Night was the time for watching when it was believed that the imps came in the form of spectres, man, women, boy, dog, cat, foal, hare, rat, toad, etc., causing all kinds of queer actions, sickness, spasms, etc., those suspected of being witches were sat on a stool, with crossed legs, and bound with cords, put in the centre of the room where they were not allowed to either eat or sleep for twenty-four hours, during which a close watch was kept for the imp to enter through a small hole in the door. When Thomas Jones was released from prison, not wishing to stay longer in America, he took passage for England aboard the ship "Welcome" that lay at anchor before Charlestown. By an odd co-incidence as soon as Jones went aboard a storm arose that caused the ship to roll. The County Court, then in session, again ordered that Jones be arrested, saying that "the ship would stand still as soon as he was in prison!" and, strange to say, as the warrant was shown to him the storm ceased. Margaret Jones was, probably, hung from a limb of the "Old Elm" on the Common. Nothing is known of the scene at the execution, except that at the same hour and on the same day a violent storm blew down many trees in Connecticut which gave more credence to the fallacies of witchcraft.

1650

The Common might be said to be a mass of rocks and bushes and mud flats, that reached far out into the water, were known as "the marsh at the bottom of the Common."

The marsh at the foot of the Common, was mostly covered with rocks and bushes, and extended from the water to above the present Park Street. There was Fox Hill, Powder House Hill, the most prominent, Flag Staff Hill, and at a later period, the Watch House.

1651 MAY 29.

The second victim of witchcraft in Boston was Mary Parsons, wife of Hugh Parsons of Springfield, who was charged with "devilish practices" on Martha and Rebecca Moxon, daughters of George Moxon a Springfield clergyman, and also for the murder of her own child. Pleading guilty to the second charge she was sentenced to be hung. The trial took place at Springfield when, after sentence, many thinking her insane, she obtained a reprieve of a few weeks. She was executed, but whether in Boston or Springfield cannot be ascertained.

OCTOBER 10.

Zacheus Bosworth sold to Thomas Millard an acre of land which was a "part of the State House lot."

William Pynchon, who arrived with Governor Winthrop's colony, returned to England where he wrote a book entitled "The Meretricious Price of our Redemption," which, creating great excitement, was denounced in the Colony as containing "many errors and heresies." When Pynchon came back to the colonies he was met every where with jeers and hisses, and, twice ordered before the court, each time refused to appear, when he abandoned the colony. The court ordered the Common hangman to burn the book on the Common.

1652

James and Peter Oliver built a wind mill on Powder House Hill, and, three years before Thomas Painter, by an annual payment of forty shillings, obtained the right to build a wind mill on Fox Hill. There were three small ponds, Frog Pond, Horse Pond and Sheehan's Pond, where cattle gathered at the foot of the hills. The largest was Frog Hill. Horse Pond, though but a small pool, slaked the thirst of many a weary animal and Sheehan's Pond, a marsh, derived its name from a criminal executed near the locality.

1653 NOVEMBER 8.

Rev. John Lathrop (Lorthropp), an "Independent Divine" died at Barnstable, Massachusetts, and was buried in the Granary Burying Ground.

1656 MARCH 31.

Gallows on the Common were ordered to be removed "to ye next Knowle."

JUNE 19.

The third execution for witchcraft in Boston was that of Mrs. Ann Hibbins, a widow, the wife of William Hibbins, a leading Boston merchant and one of the most prominent citizens of the colony. He died in 1654 having been Deputy to the General Court in 1641-2, which tried Margaret Jones, and Assistant from 1643 until his death. He was agent of the colony in England, and, being a man of wealth and culture, he and his wife moved in the most select circles of Boston. Mrs. Hibbins is also said to have been a sister of Richard Bellingham who was Governor in 1641 and Deputy Governor when her life was forfeited by her delusion. It would seem strange that her high social position could not have shielded her from her fate, and, again, no evidence can be found by which she was convicted. On her first trial in 1655 the verdict was set aside, and again, May 14th, the next year, she was brought before the General Court where, called to the bar, she declared her perfect willingness to be "tried by God and the Court!" Found guilty of witchcraft the Governor pronounced her sentence—"to go from the bar to the place from whence she came, and from thence to the place of execution, and there to hang till she was dead."

Not one of the jury, who tried Mrs. Hibbins, resided in Boston which shows plainly that no local prejudice affected the verdict. It was said that her husband's pecuniary losses had so reduced his estate that she became ugly and quarrelsome, which caused church discipline and made her odious to the neighbors so that she was accused of witchcraft, while public clamor had much to do with her conviction. Mrs. Hibbins was, also, probably hung from the same limb of the "Old Elm." Nothing is said about the scene of the locality, but after the execution a search was made in her chests and boxes for puppets, images or any articles of sorcery, but nothing was found. Her death produced feelings both of sympathy and satisfaction, some saying she was a saint and some a witch. Mrs. Hibbins was twice married, her former husband was a gentleman named Moore and by whom she had three sons all residing in England. The youngest son on hearing of his mother's misfortune came to Boston and probably saw her before her death. Her will is alluded to as a "calm, well worded and sensible document." It is found in the *Suffolk Probates,* dated May 27th, 1656, and is appraised at £344 and 14s. Its inventory mentions a diamond and gold wedding ring, a taffetty cloake, silk gown and kirtle, pink colored petticoat, etc. Thomas Clarke, Edward Hutchinson, William Hudson, Joshua Scottow, and Peter Oliver are appointed as Overseers and Administrators. Thomas Clarke was a Deputy in the General Court. Joshua Scottow and Peter Oliver were Selectmen and the rest all well known Boston citizens. She adds in a "codicial" "I do earnestly desire my loving friends Captain (Edward) Johnson, Mr. Edward Rawson to be added to the rest of the gentlemen mentioned as Overseers to my will to whom I commit, namely, to Captain Johnson's care and trust my two chests and desk with all things therein, to be kept entirely whole and in kind, till my eldest son John, or his order, authenticated by a public notary, who shall come and demand the same." Mr. Rawson was the

Secretary of the General Court and to his charge she delivered the keys of her chest and desk, and also her private papers. And of her burial, she says, "My desire is that all my overseers would be pleased to show so much respect for my dead corpse, as to cause it to be decently interred, and, if it may be, near my late husband." Learning of her son's expected arrival three days before her execution,—"I give my son Jonathan £20, over and above what I have already given him, towards his pains and charge in coming to see me, which shall be the first paid out of my estate." And again, on the morning of her execution, she adds, "My further mind and will is (sic) out of my sense of the more than ordinary affection and pains of my son Jonathan in the time of my distress, I give him, as a further legacy £10." The high standing of those chosen to administer the affairs of Mrs. Hibbins shows her station in life, while the expressions of gratitude to her friends is a clear proof that efforts were made to save her from her awful end on the gallows. Her execution was loudly denounced by the pulpit.

Matoonas, one of King Philips Sagamores, was tied to a tree and shot on the Common.

1659 March 16.

William Ledro the fourth victim was hung on the Common for being a Quaker.

October 20.

The early persecution of the Quakers in Boston led to many arrests and several executions. People were thrown into prison, their faces blackened, or publicly whipped in the Market Place. William Robinson and

Marmaduke Stevenson, both of whom had emigrated from Yorkshire, England, and Mary Dyer, an Anti nomian, of Rhode Island, were sentenced to be hanged on the Common. The hanging was done under the order of Chief Marshall Edward Michelson of Cambridge. The only authority regarding the locality is found in an old record which says "I suppose the branch of the tree was the gallows." Perhaps the "Great Tree" near the Frog Pond. Robinson and Stevenson, during their confinement, wrote a warning dated, "In the Common Gaol, in the bloody town of Boston, the 6th month, 1659," and which began, "Hearken and give ear, thou town of Boston, lend an ear, O ye Rulers, Chief Priests and Inhabitants thereof! Listen all you that dwell therein, Rich and Poor, small and great, high and low, Bond and Free, of what sort so ever, give ear, etc." Robinson also wrote a short exhortation, dated, "In the Hole of the Condemned, in Boston Gaol, the 16th day of the 8th month, 1659."

Robinson and Stevenson walked to the gallows while the sound of drums drowned their voices as they endeavored to speak. Rev. John Wilson denounced the culprits until the last moment, when both men met their death with cheerfulness and composure and embraced each other in parting. When the "stiff" bodies were cut down they fell to the ground breaking Robinson's skull, their shirts were ripped open and the bodies cast into a hole. A friend, Nicholas Upsal—caused a fence to be put up around the hole which prevented the bodies from being devoured by wild beasts, and which, uncovered, soon filled with stagnant water. Mary Dyer also ascended the ladder when, with arms and legs tied and the rope drawn 'round her neck, her son earnestly pleaded in her behalf when she was liberated. As the crowd were returning the "draw" of the bridge fell killing a woman and seriously injuring several others, which the Quakers said was an act of providence on the "wrongfully persecuted." Mary Dyer was banished from the colony.

1660 MAY 30.

The General Court passed an order which gave the almost exclusive control of the Common to the Selectmen of the Town.

The Common was bounded on the north by Beacon Street, the Granary Burying Ground and Sentry (afterward Park) Street. On the south by the open pastures on the north side of Frog Lane, (Boylston Street), and southwest by the west side of the burial ground and ran nearly parallel with Carver Street as far as water.

JUNE 1.

Mary Dyer "persuaded that her death was necessary returned the next year and delivering herself to Governor Endicott against the wishes of the Court" was also hanged on the Common. She was led to the scaffold by a number of armed men led by John Webb who, with some others, engaged in killing a whale, shortly afterwards, was carried out to sea and drowned. It was said of them "Mary Dyer whom your barberous hands slew and hung upon a tree." She was also alluded to as a "true and noble woman whose only offence was pleading the cause of religious freedom." She left a family and lies buried in some unknown place on the Common. Her husband owned an estate.

"Old Jethro," an Indian, and some Quakers are also thought to have been hung on the Common.

The first almshouse in Boston was built on the corner of Park and Beacon Streets, on the Common. It was burned twenty years afterwards and was rebuilt in 1686, two stories in height with a gambrel roof, and a wing added for better accommodation. Urchins were often seen begging outside the fence. Besides an almshouse it was also used for a hospital and insane asylum.

The old Granary Burying Ground was first started.

The waste land, extending from the almshouse to the burial ground, was taken for a second burial place on the Common.

Cows grazed on the Common.

1661

A fatal accident occurred to General Humphrey Atherton who, while returning home on horseback at night struck a cow, in the darkness, on the Common and was thrown from his horse and killed.

Rules prohibited mowing grass, or digging sods, on the Common, though gravel was dug on Fox hill, the present location of the Public Garden. Permission was also granted to fetch sand, or clay, from the same hill.

Besides the Great Elm tree there was the Tyburn Tree with a synonymous history.

1662 JANUARY 26.

An earthquake doing considerable damage in town was felt on the Common.

OCTOBER 18.

King Philip, chief of the tribe, visited Boston and the Common.

1663 TUESDAY, MAY 28.

John Josselyn, Gentleman, again visited Boston remaining in the country over eight years. Of his departure from England he writes:—"Anno 1663, May the three and twentieth, I went down to Gravesend, it being Saturday; I lay ashore till Monday, the fifth, about eleven o'clock at night I went aboard the Society (a ship) belonging to Boston, in the Massachusetts Colony of English in New England, of 200 and 20 tun, carrying sixteen iron guns, most (of them) unserviceable, manned with thirty-three sailors, and seventy-seven passengers; men, women and children." The voyage was uneventful as the only incidents noted are a shoal of turtles forty inches in extent, the finding of a shallop from Jamaica containing a crew of ten men, nearly famished, and the meeting of a Plymouth vessel, when ten weeks out—laden with cloth, fruit and honey, bound for Boston.........

The six and twentieth we had sight of land, the seven and twentieth we anchored at Nantascot. In the afternoon I went on board of a ketch, with some of our passengers, in hope to get to Boston that night, but the Master of the ketch would not consent." Of his arrival in Boston, he writes,—"The eight and twentieth being Tuesday, in the morning about five o'clock he lent us his shallop and three of his men, who brought us to the western end of the town where we landed, and having gratified (satisfied) the men, we repaired to an ordinary (for so they called taverns there), where we were provided with a liberal cup of burnt Madeira wine, and store of plum cake. About ten o'clock I went about my affairs."

Mr. Josselyn stayed in and around Boston until September (during which period the Dutch Governor of New Netherlands visited the Town, receiving the hospitality of the Governor and Magistrates and visited the Common). He then went to the house of his brother at Black Point. His first visit to Boston, on his final return to England, he describes thus: "Boston is built on the southwest side of a bay large enough for the anchorage of 500 sail of ships. The buildings are handsome, joyning one to the other as in London, with many large streets, most of them paved with pebblestone. In the high street, towards the Common, there are fair buildings; some of stone, and at the east end of the Town, one amongst the rest, built by the shore, by Mr. Gibs (probably Mr. Benjamin Gibbs) a merchant, being a stately edifice, which, it is thought, will stand him in little less than £3000, before it is fully finished. The Town is not divided into parishes, yet they have three fair meeting houses of churches, which hardly suffice to receive the inhabitants and strangers that come in from all parts.

"Having refreshed myself here for some time, and opportunely lighting upon a passage in a bark belonging to a friend of my brother's, and bound to the eastward, I put to sea again; and on the fifteenth of August I arrived at Black Point, otherwise called Scarborow, the habitation of my beloved brother, being about an hundred leagues to the eastward of Boston. Here I resided eight years, and made it my business to discover all along the natural, physical and chryrurgical rarities of this new found world."

Again he says, "The passage from Boston to Charlestown is by a ferry, worth £40 or £50 a year."

His time had been passed in scientific research, taking no part in political agitations. He returned to London in the same vessel, the New Supply, now commanded by Captain Fairweather, at the close of 1671. Mr. Josselyn, in alluding to Boston, on his last voyage, quotes from the work of Captain Johnson, thus: "The houses are for the most part raised on the sea banks, and wharfed out with great industry and cost; many of them standing upon piles, close together on each side of the street, as in London, and furnished with many fair shops. Their materials are brick, stone, lime, handsomely contrived, with three meeting houses, or churches, and a Town house, built upon pillars, where the merchants may confer. In the chambers above they keep their monethly Courts. The town is rich and populous. On the south there is a small, but pleasant, Common, where the Gallants, a little before sunset, walk with their Marmalet-madams, as we do in Morefields, till the nine o'clock bell rings them home to their respective habitations. When presently, the Constables walk their rounds to see good order kept, and to take up the people."

The Common was the beauty and pride of the Town, ever suggesting the lighter side of life.

1668

The Hancock family claimed to have planted the "Old Elm."

1669

Thomas Millard died bequeathing "a small parcel of land on the side of the Century Hill and fronting the Common." This included nearly all the State House lot.

1670

An Indian was hung on the Common, for the murder of Zachary Smith in Dedham woods.

A tradition, says, that the "Old Elm" was set out by Hezekiah Henchman, or his father Daniel at an earlier period.

Copeley's, west of Beacon Hill, on the Common.

1672 DECEMBER 7.

Governor Bellingham died and was buried in the Granary Burying Ground. He was Governor for ten years and on the day he died. When the family became extinct the tomb was given to Governor James Sullivan who found it "partly filled with water and the coffin and remains of the Governor floating around in the ancient vault" after being buried for nearly a century. Shurtleff says, "a hundred years form a strong period for such a kind of navigation." He lived on Tremont Street and died at the age of eighty-four.

Across the Neck a long ditch ran with brick wall where cannon pointed through embrasures. Sentries kept watch night and day guarding the town from any attack by the Indians.

West, a spur of Beacon Hill, on the Common.

1673

John Turner sold to Samuel Shrimpton a small strip of land (23 x 180) leading up from the Training Field to Centry Hill.

1675 SEPTEMBER 22.

John Littlejohn was hung, on the Common, for murder.

Some Indians captured in St. Philip's War were hung on the Common. The hangman was Chief Marshall Edward Michelson.

1676 JULY 27.

Old Matoonas, who, with 160 of his tribe, surrendered in the Indian War was "bound with cords," and charged with the first murder in the Massachusetts Colony, was brought into Boston and condemned to death. His betrayer "Sagamore John," who had connived the surrender, and his men were made executioners. "Old Matoonas" was led to the Common where, tied to a tree, he was shot. His father was hung several years previously.

AUGUST.

About thirty Indian prisoners of war were hung on the Common.

NOVEMBER 27.

The largest fire that had ever happened in Boston destroyed much property. It was caused by a boy carelessly setting a candle and going to sleep. The flames started at the Red Lion Tavern an hour before day light, and raging three or four hours, destroyed five dwellings, several warehouses, the Second Church, and Increase Mather's house. A strong southeast wind, which changed to the south, caused the flames to spread over a wide space (Richmond, Hanover and Clark Streets) as far as the water. Buildings were blown up and a heavy rainfall prevented further damage, otherwise the whole south end of the town would have been laid in ashes. Many saved their household effects by carrying them to the Common.

1677

A second burial place was started on the Common.

1678

Nine Indians were shot on Windmill Hill.

Permission was given to John Woodmansey to use the burial ground on the Common as a pasture.

Sewall's Diary says: "A whipping post is set by the middle Watch House" on the Common, where many suffered for various offences.

1680

The Green Dragon Tavern on Union Street, a few steps from Hanover, was built about this year, and was long an old landmark. During the Revolution Samuel Adams, James Otis, Joseph Warren, Paul Revere and other patriots held meetings within its walls. Its lodgers came to the Common.

1681

John Turner died when his executor was empowered to sell his "house and land on the upper end of the

Common or Training Field, and the land on Beacon Hill."

Colonel Samuel Shrimpton bought a side of Beacon Hill running a passage from the Common.

1683 OCTOBER 5.

Hon. John Hull "Mint Master," died, and was buried in the "Hull Tomb" in the Granary Burying Ground. He was treasurer of the Colony and coined the celebrated New England shillings.

1684

A clause in the city charter prevented the Common and Faneuil Hall from ever being sold.

1685 APRIL 3.

News of the death of King Charles II was much talked about in town and on the Common.

Judge Sewall writes that "a Quaker or two" went to the Governor to get permission to surround the ground with pales, under the gallows, where the quakers were buried. The Governor refused the plea to the Council, who denied the request thinking it "very convenient" for any such persons "so dead and buried" to be so designated.

1686 MARCH 11.

James Morgan—a murderer, was hung on the Common. Some came a distance of fifty miles to witness the execution which was the first in seven years. Morgan had threatened a man that, if he came inside his door, he "wou'd run the spit into his bowels!" which he did. The prison, where Morgan was kept, is described as a "house of meagre looks and ill smells, for lice, drink, and tobacco are the compound, or if you will, too the suburbs of hell, and the persons much the same as these."

1688 JANUARY 9.

Mr. Sampson Sheafe was attacked, knocked down and robbed, by two ruffians, on the Common. A man named Humbleton, who was present, it was thought instigated the act.

JUNE 9.

Another account says:

Lawrence Hammond says in his diary; "this evening Mr. Sampson Sheafe was set upon in Boston Common, and knocked down and robbed by two ruffiians. One Humbleton being present, who, it is judged, hired them to do it." Robbers and highwaymen had not entirely disappeared from the Common.

NOVEMBER 5.

Pope's Day—effigies were (as always) burned and bonfires blazed on the Common, where precautions were taken that no injury should be done to the trees.

NOVEMBER 16.

The fourth and last execution for witchcraft in Boston was the woman Goody Glover who was hung, probably from the "Old Elm" on the Common. She was charged with imparting the spell of witchery to the four children of John Goodwin a "sober and pious" Mason who lived in South Boston. The records of this execution are probably more complete than any of the rest as Cotton Mather bares the circumstances in his Memorable Providences" in 1689. It was regarded as the most alarming of any of the cases. The children, all of a docile and sweet disposition, had been reared in the religious forms of the Colonial period. The eldest, a girl of thirteen or fourteen, had said the laundress had taken family linen, whereupon the mother of the servant, an Irish woman of bad character, used insulting language to the girl resulting in her having diabolical fits. A sister and two brothers also showed alarming symptoms, and, similarly tormented, were kept in separate rooms, none being aware of the condition of the others. At intervals they were deaf, dumb and blind, and, at other times, all three disorders would appear together. "Their tongues would be drawn their throats, then pulled out upon their chins, their jaws, necks, shoulders, elbows and all their joints would appear to be dislocated, and they would make the most piteous outcries of burning, being cut with knives, beat, etc." Joshua Moody, Minister of the First Church, says: "The children would also show torments in their head, eyes, tongue, teeth, breaking their neck, back, thighs, knees, legs, feet, toes, etc., and then would roar out: 'O' my head! O' my neck!' etc. And, it is also said, they would 'bark like dogs, purr like cats,' and complain that they were 'punched,' 'pricked,' 'pulled' or 'cut.' A day of fasting and prayer was appointed in Boston and Charlestown for the children when the youngest child recovered. The other three remained 'bewitched.' When the woman was arrested and, who refusing to either affirm or deny the charges, met her death saying that the children would "never be relieved."

During the trial of Goody Glover small images or

puppets made of rags and stuffed with goat's hair were found in her house and shown in the court room when she wet her finger and stroking the image, said it was her procedure of venting her anger on victims. When asked if she had a friend to appear in her behalf, she, at first, replied "Yes!" but gazing upward, said, "No, he is gone!" Cries were heard at night toward a devil, with whom she had communed, for deserting her. During her confinement in jail Goody Glover was visited by Cotton Mather, grandson of the "Great Cotton," who assisted his father in the pastorate of the North Church in Boston, and who, after the execution, took the three children to his house where they all recovered through the "efficacy of prayer."

1689 FRIDAY, JANUARY 17.

Two pirates were condemned, at the Town House, to be hanged on the Common.

JANUARY 17.

Sewall says, in his "Diary"; that, in company with Cotton Mather, he visited the Pirates, who, convicted on that day, were afterward hung on the Common.

JANUARY 27.

Captain James Hawkins and seven Pirates were hung on the Common.

APRIL 18.

Soon after Sir Edmund Andros had assumed the charge of the government the use of Beacon Hill became a matter of public discussion when it was declared that the Beacon Hill had not been erected to guard against the Indians, but against the local authorities whom, it was deemed, had oppressed the people since the old charter was rescinded. Andros claimed that the Peninsula then reverted to the King. This created a widespread indignation among the settlers, who maintained that the householders of Boston were entitled to the land by the Blackstone purchase, and besides that in 1684-5 they had also settled an Indian claim to the Peninsula, when Andros declared that an Indian signature bore no more legal meaning than the "scratch of a bear's claw." The Andros rebellion followed and the people all rose in arms, drums beat throughout the town and an ensign was displayed from the Beacon and, when the rebellion closed, the "Jack" was hoisted up at the Fort and the colors again waving at Beacon Hill, notified a thousand soldiers at Charlestown that all was over and prevented an assemblage on the hill. The governor had surrendered the government and the castle to the people. No blood had been shed in the two days of anarchy, though Andros was taken to Fort Hill and who, with Mr. Dudley, Mr. Randolph the instigator of the rebellion—and other persons, was imprisoned through the summer and fall and then sent to England to be tried, but all escaped punishment. It was said that Andros first inspired the colonists to resist an oppressive and unjust government.

April 18.

The colonists having suffered many restrictions when it was rumored in Boston that William had ascended the throne, and that full liberties would be restored, there was a grand celebration on the Common.

PROVINCIAL PERIOD

1692

A New Charter changed the colony into the "Province of Massachusetts." The Common was now carefully watched by the board of Selectmen, holes were filled and stagnant water drained.

The cellar foundation of the house of Samuel Sewall was laid by stone and rocks taken from the Common.

1693 August 27.

Edward Rawson, Secretary of the Colony, died in Boston, and was buried in the Granary Burying Ground.

1697 March 22.

A Town ordinance prevented any person "riding to and fro" to water their horses, on the Common, on the "Sabbath Day." A fine, so incurred, would be five shillings. Mr. Daniel Fairfield was fully authorized to enforce this law.

December 12.

Rev. "Jon" Baily died, and was buried in the Granary Burying Ground. He came to Boston in 1692 and became pastor of the First Church a year afterward, where he remained until he died at the age of fifty-three. "A faithful minister of the Gospel in Boston."

Whittier's poem, "The Prophecy of Samuel Sewall—1697," contains the lines:

"Stately and low, with thoughtful air,
His black cap hiding his whitened hair,
Walks the Judge of the great Assize,
Samuel Sewall, the good and wise.

When he sat on the bench at the witchcraft courts,
With the laws of Moses and Hale's Reports;
And spake, in the name of both, the word
That gave the witches' neck to the cord."

Whittier's poem also contains the lines:

"Up and down the Village streets
Strange are the forms my fancy meets.

The ancient worthies I see again.
I hear the tap of the elder's cane,
And his awful periwig I see,
And the silver buckles of shoe and knee."

1698

The pasture adjoining Beacon Hill, owned by the widow of Samuel Shrimpton, was appraised at £150. This included the location of the State House and about two acres to the north.

Close of the 17th Century.

Two duels were fought on the Common. The first was between Peggy and Captain Cole, the other occurred several years afterward. The duellists were each fined £10.

During the ravages of the small-pox the clothes of the victims were spread out on a place in the Common during the night, and many who had died of the dread disease were buried in the Common, or Granary Burying Ground.

The Common was always a playground for boys—wicket and flinging of the bullit was much enjoyed. Flinging the bullit was finally prohibited as dangerous to pedestrians who chanced to be passing. No games were allowed to be played on the Sabbath, and a fine of five shillings was imposed on the owner of any horse seen on the Common on that day. People were not even to stroll on the Common, during the warm weather, on Sunday.

During the week the Common presented a gala sight by persons walking and riding with children at play.

There was a landing on the shore where people crossed over from Cambridge. Sewall wrote: "Rode to commencement, had a pleasant passage home by water with Mr. Wendell and his family. Landed at the bottom on the Common.

In a series of letters written in Boston, reviewing the early period in 1855 "Gleaner" says, "We have inspected the hogs in Hog Alley (running out of Washington Street) and the cows on the Common."

Frog Lane, named from the croakers heard at nightfall, is now called Boylston Street, but which is now proposed to call Squirrel Avenue.

1700 JANUARY 2.

"Sewall's Diary," says:—The beginning of the century "At break of day Jacob Amsden, and three other trumpeters, stood, near Mr. Alfords, and blew a loud blast on the Common. Then went to the Green Chamber, and sounded there till sunrise."

The maps of Boston give some idea of the Common in its early days.

1702 MAY 28.

Proclamation of Queen Anne caused much talk on the Common.

1703 APRIL 26.

George Ripley was appointed to the charge of watering the bulls and driving them into the burial place at night.

MAY.

A sentry box was built on the Common.

1704 JUNE.

John Quelch and five companions, all pirates, were hung at low tide, on the Neck, at Charles River.

The Almshouse was repaired—by Mr. Thrasher, on the Common.

1706

Spinning became an industry for the inmates of the almshouse and workhouse.

The Powder house—built this year—was watched by two men who, nightly, walked twice over the Common, special caution being taken on holidays. The powder was carried, in covered boats, across the river to the landing at the bottom of the Common. A watch house was also built on the adjoining hill.

The South Burying Ground, that adjoined the Workhouse, on the Common where soldiers were mostly buried during the seige.

1707

Rev. Samuel Willard,—"the eminent divine," and pastor of the Old South Church, died, and was buried in the Granary Burying Ground.

1708 MAY 3.

A "Description of Boston" (1807) says, "Certain streets, lanes, and alleys, were recorded, boundaries and names: The upper part of Washington Street was called Orange Street, and is spoken of as "the broad street or highway from the old fortifications on the neck leading into the town, as far as the corner of the late Deacon Elliott's house."

"The way leading easterly from said Elliott's corner,

by the late Deacon Allen's extending to Windmill pond —Essex Street."

The way leading from Captain Frary's corner, westward to the bottom of the Common, with a turn southerly down to the sea in Frog Lane (Boylston Street).

"Hog Alley, from Newbury Street, westerly, to the Common."

"Sea Street, from Ball's corner to Windmill point."

"Beacon Street, from Mr. Whitcomb's corner through the upper side of the Common, and down to the sea."

1709

Paul Mascarene, who commanded a new artillery company, built small earth works at the foot of the Common and drilled his men in the various artillery movements.

1712

Trees were ordered planted along the burying ground.

1713 April 21.

The Selectmen for the sum of 40s allowed James Williams the grass of the burial ground and who was to be responsible for any damage done to the graves by the cows.

May 20.

A riot—says Sewall in his "Diary"—was caused "by two hundred people, or more, breaking open Arthur

Mason's warehouse in the Common thinking to find corn there."

SEPTEMBER 13.

David Wallace was hung, on the Common, for murder.

OCTOBER 8.

Permission was given to Thomas Bannister to build a barn, with a flat roof, on the beach at the lower end of the Common.

LIFE AND TIMES OF BENJAMIN FRANKLIN.

by

JAMES PARTON,

(1864)

"An anecdote is preserved of Benjamin's minnow fishing days. There was a marsh in the outskirts of Boston, on the edge of which the boy and his friends used to fish at high tide for minnows. By much trampling the spot having been made a mere quagmire, Franklin proposed to construct a wharf for the boys to stand upon and pointed out a large heap of stones intended for a new house near by, which, he said, would answer their purpose perfectly. Accordingly, in the evening when the workmen were gone home, he assembled his playfellows, and very soon the wharf was completed." pp. 39.

"Franklin, upon the whole, spent a very happy boyhood, and his heart yearned for Boston as long as he lived. When he was eighty-two years old, he spoke of it as 'that beloved place.' He said, in the same letter, that he would dearly like to ramble again over the scene of so many innocent pleasures; and as that could not be, he had a singular pleasure in the company and conversation of its inhabitants. 'The Boston manner,' he touchingly added, 'the turn of phrase, and even the tone of voice and accent and pronunciation all please, and seem to revive and refresh me.' "

"If Franklin could now revisit the scenes of his boyhood, there is still there one object which he would recognize, besides the beautiful harbor and its emerald isles, the great elm on Boston Common was "The Great Elm" when Benjamin Franklin played under it in boyhood, and drove home, at sunset, his father's cow from the Common around Beacon Hill." pp. 51.

1715 MAY 21.

The French Protestants who, after the revocation of the edict of Nantes, sought refuge in Boston, selected a place for interments in the Granary Burying Ground. Among their number laid to rest was a "beloved minister"—Pierre Daillé. The worn headstone was found by some laborers, excavating a cellar on Pleasant Street, nearly a century and a half afterwards. It bore the inscription: "Here lyes ye body of ye Reverend Mr. Peter Daillé, Minister of ye French Church in Boston —Died the 21st of May, 1715, in the 67th year of his age." When he died all the clergy of the town without regard to sect, were given gloves and scarfs.

JUNE 4.

Margaret Callahan was hung on the Common for murder.

Shrimpton owned Beacon Hill. Thompson owned land on the Common.

1717 JULY 29.

Permission was given to Patrick Ogilvie, of Boston, Marriner, to build a dwelling house, with a kitchen to adjoin, on the lower end of the Common.

Tombs were allowed to be built in the Granary Burying Ground.

The straightening of the Mall separated it from the burying ground.

1718

An attempt was made by Colonel Dalrymple of the Fourteenth Royal Regulars, to obtain the Spinning School Building, on the site of the Scollay's Building, for "quarters." This was firmly resisted by the tenants headed by Elisha Brown. When the Sheriff and his officers came with a mandate from Governor Bernard they were compelled to gain entrance by the cellar where they were kept as prisoners until released by a file of soldiers from the Common.

Some of the spinners wore garments of their own make showing their skill and industry.

Captain Thomas Smart and John Boydell fought a duel, on the Common, one forenoon, resulting in one being shot in the arm. The duellists were arrested, fined, and imprisoned for one day.

Northern Lights alarmed the inhabitants of the town and on the Common.

1719 APRIL 29.

It was ordered that the South Burying Ground be enlarged next to the "Common and Training Field."

MAY 15.

The first Aurora Borealis ever seen in Boston was observed by many on the Common.

1720

Owing to the enlargement of the Workhouse on the Common, the Pound was removed from the burying ground near (Tremont Street) to the site of the Park Street Church.

A children's spinning school was started on a neighborhood street. A number of Irish persons had come from Londonderry who showed great skill in the machine which was worked by the foot. Spinning wheels were brought into the Common and worked by the "females of the town" all vying with each other to attain the greatest speed.

The Common was the cherished possession of Boston.

1721

The Bridewall on the Common was occasionally used for lunatics.

1722

The size of the "Old Elm" on the Common makes it appear that it existed before the settlement of Boston.

1723 AUGUST 23.

The game of "throwing the long bullits" on the Common was forbidden by law and no person was permitted to dig sand, earth or stones at Fox Hill, or the Ridge between Fox and Windmill Hills.

AUGUST 25.

Aquitamong, an Indian, 112 years old, visited Boston and went to the Common.

Some Indian delegates to Boston lived in an encampment on the Common. The *Boston News-Letter,* says "Said delegates had an ox given to them on Friday last which they killed with Bow and Arrows, and in the evening a fire was made in the Common, and a Kettle hung over it, in which part of said Ox was boiled, where they danced after their own manner, in presence of some of our principal gentlemen and also some thousands of spectators."

1724 AUGUST 1.

The ascension of George I to the throne was celebrated in Boston and on the Common.

1726 JUNE 12.

William Fly, and his two companions, Samuel Cole and Henry Greenville were hung at Charlestown Ferry for piracy, Fly, the ring leader, was hung in irons at Nixs Mate where he was left dangling as a warning for spectators. The other two were buried in the gravel on the bank, at low tide.

1727 OCTOBER 29.

An earthquake, rocking the houses in town, was felt on the Common.

Ezekial Lewis and James Williams were allowed the sum of 26s-8d, a third of the yearly rental of the South Burying Ground, as they had lost a part of their feed which was caused by a broken fence.

The General Court passed laws prohibiting swimming or walking on the highways, fields, or the Common, under a penalty of being put in jail, "set in the stocks," etc.

1728 JULY 3.

The first duel in Boston was fought, on the Common, between Henry Phillips and Benjamin Woodbridge both belonging to prominent families. The young men, who were intimate friends, had quarrelled over a game of cards, or wine, at the Royal Exchange Tavern, a noted resort for those of sportive habits, in town, which resulted in a challenge. The parties, with their seconds, proceeded to a secluded spot (the site of the Powder House) where they met, in a deadly encounter, under the moonlight, swords being used for weapons. Woodbridge was mortally wounded! while Phillips, who, with a slight wound, was hurried away by his brother Gillam and Peter Faneuil aboard the man-o-war *Sheerness* and sailed for France where he died of grief at Rochelle within the year. Phillips was a Harvard graduate, aged 24. Woodbridge was buried in the Granary Burying Ground where a tablet is inscribed: "In the 20th year of his age." He was a son of "Dudley Woodbridge, Esq." a Barbadoes merchant and partner of Jonathan Sewall. The affair created much excitement.

JULY.

The Governors had experienced much difficulty in getting their "small pittance" of a salary which they were allowed by the General Court. To meet this difficulty an act was signed for the issue of £50,000 in bills of credit. Governor Burnet was escorted into Boston with a large parade and much ceremony, and, impressed with the "plenty of this great province," urged the passage of the bill. This created much interest in the town and on the Common.

The Granary, or meal house, Francis Willoughby, keeper, was a long wooden building capable of holding 1200 bushels of grain which was sold, at a low price, to the poor who came from all parts of the town, and which continued until the end of the Revolution. The Granary and the Workhouse led to the Granary (formerly the south) Burying Ground which—on the outskirts of the town, opened on and was originally a part of the Common. It was named for the Old Granary, and, preceded by King's Chapel and Copps Hill, was the third cemetery of Boston.

Two boys, George and Nathan Howell, were drowned while skating on the "Back Bay," where the Public Garden now stands, a favorite skating locality. The sad accident created widespread regret.

Trees were planted in front of the Granary Burying Ground forming a pathway called the "Little Mall."

A row of elms was planted on the Common.

1730 JANUARY 1.

Chief Justice Samuel Sewall, known as the "Witches Judge" and the author of the famous "Diary," died, and was buried in the Granary Burying Ground. "A very high character for learning, piety and humility; for justice, benevolence and compassion."

1733 MARCH.

It was ordered that care should be taken of the trees on the Common and another row be planted and also that a row of posts be set up with a rail on top.

1734 MARCH.

It was resolved that "the row of trees already planted on the Common, should be taken off by the Selectmen," who were also instructed to plant another row, and also to erect a row of posts, surmounted by a rail, to extend "through the Common from the Granary Burial Place to Colonel Fitche's fence, leaving openings at the several streets and lanes." Five years elapsed, however, before the fence separated the Granary Burying Ground from the Common, when, in 1739, a fence was set up from Common Street to Beacon. The fence, many times renewed stood until 1836 when it was replaced by an iron one at a cost of $82,159 and 85 cents. The stone foundation cost $5,000—$16,292 was raised by private contributions. Its length is 5932 feet—or a mile and an eighth, and covers a circuit of 48⅜ acres. The Common contains 50 acres.

A second row of elms was planted on the Common.

1735

John Alford sold to Thomas Hancock, "a lot near Beacon Hill, bounded, se. by the Common. Hancock paid £1,000 for this acre where the Hancock mansion was built.

The Common received its first proper fence enclosure.

1737 MARCH.

A committee, composed of several residents appointed by the farm, recommended Common Street where the Granary stood, as a location for a Workhouse. The Granary was to be removed to the corner of Tremont and Common Streets.

The Common was separated from the Granary by a fence, running up the hill, which in two years was extended to Beacon Street.

Thirty loads of sand were permitted to be taken from Fox Hill to be used in the erection of the Workhouse which stood partly on the locality of the Granary which was moved farther down the Hill.

Many persons from Roxbury and Cambridge landed on the wharf, at the foot of the Common, where many dug sand and obtained stones with which to build.

The neighboring land, owned by Mr. Foster, was subsequently added to the Common.

A stone house, the first built on Beacon Hill was the home of Thomas Hancock, a wealthy Boston merchant and an uncle of General Hancock. It stood a little below the summit.

The old stone Hancock mansion, on Beacon Street, opposite the Common, was demolished.

1738

The Workhouse, for the vagrant and dissolute was 140 feet longer than the Almshouse.

1739

It was ordered to "set a row of posts and rails, from Common Street up to Beacon Street, to prevent carts, etc., from spoiling the herbage of the Common.

The ground near the Winter Street entrance was raised to prevent water running over the Common from Beacon Hill.

A declaration of war with the West Indies led to troops being formed throughout the Province. The Boston Militia drilled on the Common in the presence of many townspeople.

1740 SEPTEMBER.

Rev. George Whitefield—assistant to John Wesley in England—visited Boston where "the Common people heard him gladly." He said the town was "remarkable for the external observance of the Sabbath—men in civil offices have a regard for religion. The Governor (Belcher) encourages them; and the ministers and magistrates seem to be more united than those in any other place where I have been. I never saw so little scoffing, never had so little opposition."

During the "Great Awakening" the Puritan Clergy had invited Whitefield to come and arouse the town which they thought was then in a state of lethargy. The

Old South Church could not accommodate the crowds that flocked to hear the great preacher, then in his 26th year. People climbed upon the windows while others walked about the streets, so it was decided to hold services on the Common where both on Sundays, and week days vast assemblages gathered numbering from four to six thousand and over 20,000 at the farewell sermon. As the population of Boston was then 18,000 many evidently came from the neighboring towns. Of Whitefield's work in Boston one clergyman said that never "except at the time of the general earthquake" had the people been "so happily concerned about their souls." Another said that even "negroes and boys left their rudeness." Franklin, in his "autobiography" says; "I perceived that he intended to finish with a collection, and I silently resolved he should get nothing from me. I had in my pocket a handful of copper money, three or four silver dollars, and five pistoles in gold. As he proceeded I began to soften, and I concluded to give the coppers. Another stroke of his oratory made me ashamed of that, and determined me to give the silver; and he finished so admirably, that I emptied my pocket wholly into the collection dish, gold and all." A lady who listened to one of Whitefield's sermons delivered on the Common at sunrise, said, that after he had given the words of his text, "If I take the wings of the morning and dwell in the uttermost parts of the sea," his voice was like that of an angel when he uttered them, while his arms rose slowly from his sides with an indescribable grace. I should have felt no surprise to see him ascend into the air. That would have been no miracle. The miracle was rather that he remained on earth." He possessed marvelous power as a preacher and has probably, never been equalled in drawing those "eager to go forth to hear him." He preached twice a day.

A negro, on the outskirts of the Common during one of the services, mistook a man for Whitefield, and falling down and rolling over on the ground, exclaimed "Oh, Massa Whitefield! Massa Whitefield!" The man told the negro of his mistake, when, suddenly rising to his feet again, he said, "Oh, den I'se gone dirtied myself all for nothin'!"

SEPTEMBER 18-25.

Some idea of the crowds that flocked to hear Whitefield may be gleaned from the following account in the *Boston Weekly News-Letter,* "Last Monday in the Afternoon, the Rev'd Mr. Whitefield intending to preach in the Rev'd Mr. Checkley's Meeting House (the New South) at the South part of the town, just before the time when the Service was to begin, some Noise happened by the Breaking of a Piece of Board in one of the Gallerys (used) by some to make a seat of it; it was given out by some impudent Person, that the Gallerys gave way, (tho' there was no Danger thereof), the House being prodigiously crowded, the whole Congregation was put to the utmost confusion and Disorder, so that being in the greatest Concern how to save their Lives, some jumped off the Gallery in the Seats below, others out of the windows and those below pressing to get out of the Porch Doors in haste, several were thereby thrown down one over another, and trod upon by those that were crowding out, whereby many were exceedingly bruised and others their Bones broke. But what is most sorrowful, two married women in town, viz.: Mrs. Storey and Mrs. Ingersole, and a Servant lad were so crushed that they dyed a few minutes after; and on Tuesday Mrs. Shepard a widow of good repute in town, and Mrs. Ruggles a married woman died also of the Bruises they received by the Crowd, and some others we hear are so much hurt, that 'tis to be feared they cannot recover."

OCTOBER 9-16.

The Boston Weekly News-Letter, in "A Practical Account of the several Collections made for the Orphan House in Georgia" says of one collection, on the Common, that the sum amounted to £200 15s. 6d. The total collections during Whitefield's stay were over £2800.

1742

John Davenport, "a wonderful to search out hypocrites" preached to great multitudes on the Common. Many of his assertions, however, gave offense causing retractions.

Another duel was fought by two negroes—Cæsar and Tom—on the Common, both were arrested and tried.

1743 MARCH 3.

Peter Faneuil died, and was buried with great honor, in the Granary Burying Ground. The "cradle of liberty," where his portrait hangs on the wall, ever recalls his name, public spiritedness and generosity.

APRIL.

Fox Hill not to be dug any more.

1744

Whitefield again visited Boston when he was met at Long Wharf by Dr. Chauncy, who, disliking him, said,

"Mr. Whitefield, I am sorry to see you come back again!" When Mr. Whitefield replied: "So is the Devil!" He preached on the Common.

A seminary stood at the side of Beacon Hill.

Josiah Franklin was buried in the Granary Burying Ground.

1745 JULY 3.

The News of the surrender of Louisbourg caused great rejoicings in Boston and the event was marked by a handsome bonfire for the "less polite" and where good liquor was drank, probably on Beacon Hill.

JULY 8.

The Boston Evening Post, says: "As Captain Bennett arrived in the Night, he first carried the General and Commodores dispatches to his Excellency, then at Dorchester, and on his return communicated the joyful tidings to the Hon. Colonel Wendell's Company of Militia, then on Duty as a military Watch, who (not able longer to conceal their joy) about 4 o'clock, alarm'd the town, by firing their Guns and beating their Drums, and before fire, all the Bells in the Town began to ring, and continued ringing most part of the Day. The Inhabitants thus agreeably surprised laid aside all thoughts of Business, and each one seemed to strive to out-do his Neighbor in Expressions of Joy. Many persons who were gone to Cambridge to be present at the Commencement, came to Town to rejoice with us, as did many others from the Country, and the Day was spent in firing of Cannon, feastings, and drinking of Healths, and in preparing Fire works, etc., against the

Evening. And to add to the Pleasures of the Day, Colonel Pollard and his Company of Cadets were under Arms, and made a very fine Appearance. Now the Churl and Niggard became generous, and even the Poor forget their Poverty, and in the Evening the whole Town appeared as it were in a Blaze, almost every House being finely illuminated. In some of the principal streets were a great variety of Fireworks and curious Devices for the Entertainment of the almost numberless Spectators, and in the Fields were several Bonfires for the diversion of the less Polite, besides a large one in the Common, where was a Tent erected, and plenty of good liquor for all that would drink. In a Word, never before, upon any occasion, was observed so universal and unaffected a Joy, nor was there ever seen so many Persons of both Sexes at the Time walking about, as appeared that Evening, the Streets being as light as Day, and the weather extremely pleasant. And what is very remarkable, no ill Accident happened to any Person, nor was there any of those Disorders committed, which are too common (on) such Occasions."

An Englishman—Joseph Bennett—visited Boston and wrote of the Mall, on the northwest side of the Common, where the ladies "visit, drink tea and indulge every piece of gentility to the height of the mode, and neglect the affairs of their families with as good a grace as the first ladies in London."

1746

Apprehensions of trouble with the Mother Country, arising out of home matters, led the colonists to form troops which were drilled on the Common.

The fall of the Fortress at Louisbourg had spread a general alarm throughout the Province that a fleet, under Duke D'Anville, was on the ocean and would attack Boston when aid was summoned from the neighboring towns. Douglass wrote, in his "Memoirs of the War" that "6400 men from the Country, well armed, appeared in Boston Common, some of them, from Brookfield, travelled seventy miles in two days, each with a pack (in which was provision for fourteen days) of about a bushel of corn weight. The fleet scattered in a tempest and no attack was made.

All parts of the Common were improved for a playground.

1747 NOVEMBER.

A British squadron, off the coast, created much talk while Commodore Knowles, lying in Boston harbor, seized several inhabitants to fill his quota. An infuriated mob, in retaliation, now seized several officers of the squadron who were on shore, and, passing the Common, surrounded the Town House, demanding the General Court to obtain redress. The militia were called out, but did not obey the summons immediately, so Governor Shirley fled to the Castle. The House of Representatives, standing by the Governor "with their lives and fortunes," ordered the release of the officers, while Commodore Knowles discharged most of the men that were seized and sailed away with his squadron. A town meeting was held in Boston when it was declared that the riot had been caused by "negroes and persons of vile condition."

1749 JULY 3.

The Independent Advertiser, says: "A pasture, at the bottom of the Common, took fire......and spread over an acre of ground in a quarter of an hour; the people were obliged to pull down the fences to prevent their being burnt, having took fire."

1750 MAY 15.

It was discussed at a town meeting to remove the Powder House from the Common, when it was decided that "the town will do nothing concerning it."

Among the leading Boston families were the Prices, Chardon's, Wendell's, and Oliver's all noted by their distinction, title, blood, escutcheon and family. Nason says: "Those gentlemen and ladies who occupied the North, or Court end, of the Town, who read the Spectator, Samuel Richardson's parmela and the Prayer Book, who had manors of a thousand acres, in the country, cultivated by slaves from Africa—were many of them allied to the first families in England, and it was their chief ambition to keep up the ceremonies and customs of the aristocratic society which they represented. In those dignitaries,—who in brocaded vest, gold lace coat, broad ruffled sleeves and small clothes, with three cornered hat, and powdered wig, side arms and silver shoe buckles, promenaded Queen Street and the Mall, adjoining the Common, spread themselves through the Kings Chapel, or discovered the measures of the Pelham's, Walpole and Pitt at the Rose and Crown,—as much of aristocratic pride, as much of courtly consequence displayed itself as in the frequenters of Hyde Park or Regent Street.

In Boston it is said at this period, several families kept a coach and horses, a few drove four horses, and more kept chaises and saddle horses — *pro rata* — than in London. The roads were kept in good condition in summer though there were no turn-pikes, and that travelling was as safe at night as in the day. Highway robbers were unknown. The drives were pleasant on the Common or through the woods and past prosperous farms, houses, cottages, and gentlemen's manors between the towns. Ladies, accompanied by a negro servant, were generally seen driving in a chaise, or chairs, drawn by a single horse. Gentlemen, also with servant, drove out—English fashion, in chairs, and on horseback. The mode of travel was the same for business as for pleasure—in black equipages.

Every afternoon, after tea, gentlemen and ladies were seen walking on the Mall, and would then go to one another's house to pass the evening.

During the winter season carriages discarded the wheels and were driven on runners, when balls jingled from the horses heads, and singing, cheerfulness and mirth made an animated scene on a winter's day, when open sledges, with twenty persons, drove across the Common, or about the country.

1751 MAY 17.

A young negro was hung, on the Common, for murder.

1752

John Yeamans sold to Thomas Hancock two acres of land near Beacon Hill.

The Common did not include *all* of Beacon Hill.

Abiah Franklin—wife of Josiah—was buried in the Granary Burying Ground.

1753 AUGUST 13.

The Fourth Anniversary of an industrial society was celebrated of which the *Boston Evening Post* gives the following: "Wednesday last being the Meeting of the Society for *encouraging Industry and employing the Poor,* the Rev. Mr. Cooper of this Town, preached an excellent Sermon before *them,* and a vast Assembly of other Persons, of all Ranks and Denominations, in the Old South Meeting House, from those Words in I Corinthians, 13.5. *Charity seeketh not her own.* After sermon £453 old Tenor, was collected (besides the Subscription Money of the Society) for the further promoting of laudable undertaking. In the Afternoon, about 300 Spinners, all neatly dressed, and many of 'em Daughters of the best Families in Town, appeared on the Common and being placed orderly in three Rows, at Work, made a most delightful Appearance. The Weavers also, (cleanly dressed in Garments of their own weaving) with a Loom, and a young Man at Work, on a Stage prepared for that Purpose, carried on Men's Shoulders, attended by Musick, preceded the Society, and a long Train of other Gentlemen of Note, both of Town and Country, as they walked in Procession to view the Spinners; and the Spectators were so numerous, that they were compared by many, to one of Mr. Whitefield's Auditories, when he formerly preached here on the Common."

The "Spinning craze" was soon over.

1754 NOVEMBER 19.

William Wier was hung, on the Common, for murder.

The Common Burial Ground was purchased by Mr. Andrew Oliver.

1755 NOVEMBER 18.

An earthquake which threw down the vane on Faneuil Hall and demolished ten chimneys was felt on the Common.

1756 JUNE 2.

Some sextons were ordered to remove some poisonous weeds in the burying ground near the Almshouse.

The Common Burying Ground was started. It was known at various times as the South and Central Ground. Tradition asserts that it was first used for negro burials, though it is well known that British, who died of disease, were buried there, and also soldiers who died of wounds received at the Battle of Bunker Hill, who were buried in a trench, many of whom were exhumed in the sub-excavations in the northwest corner of the yard.

The Granary Burying Ground having become crowded, bodies being sometimes buried four deep—and neglected, the authorities purchased a portion of Colonel Fitche's pasture at the foot of the Common. This was the South Burying Ground and afterwards known as the Common and Central Ground. Burials were frequently made, however, in the Granary.

The Ropewalks, on the Common, were used as stables, by the British, and the Old South Church as a riding school.

1759

The town added the portion occupied by the Central Burying Ground to the Common.

1758 MAY 17.

The Selectmen gave John Ramstead the herbage of the burying ground, for one year, for £3, 6s. 8d.

MONDAY, SEPTEMBER 18.

At the close of the "Old French War" about 4500 men commanded by General Jeffry Amherst, pitched tents on the Common. The *Boston Evening Post,* says: "Between 30 and 40 transports which came up under Convoy of the Captain (of the) Man of War are also arrived, having on board the 2nd Battalion of Royal Scots, General Forbes, Lascelle's and Webb's Regiments, and also Frazer's Highlanders. They arrived here in good Health, and were encamped on the Common; and on Saturday Morning they decamped and proceeded on the March for Lake George.

OCTOBER 22.

Rev. Thomas Prince, pastor of the Old South Church, died, and was buried in the Granary Burying Ground.

1759

The troops that conquered Quebec were recruited by Amherst, on the Common.

1760 DECEMBER 25.

News of the death of George II caused much regret in Boston and on the Common.

1761 OCTOBER 10.

Governor Dummer died in Boston, aged eighty-two years, and was buried in the Granary Burying Ground. "He preserved an unspotted character through life."

1765 AUGUST 13.

A body of citizens, organizing as the "Sons of Liberty," met under the branches of a tree which they named Liberty Tree.

The Liberty Tree stood at the corner of (the present) Washington and Essex Streets.

AUGUST 13.

An effigy of Mr. Oliver, who distributed stamps in Boston, was hung, from the Liberty Tree, with Satan, holding a scroll in his claw, peering from a boat, decrying Lord Bute who advocated the "stamp act" in Parliament.

NOVEMBER 1.

The Stamp Act to go into effect. The bells were tolled, Minute guns fired and flags hung at half-mast from the vessels that lay anchored in the harbor. Children, passing along the Common shouted the familiar, motto, "Liberty, Property, No Stamps."

The Gun House was built on the Common.

Two rival parties in Boston, who, in celebrating, marched through the streets, and to gain possession of the trophies, would end the day in a fight near Mill Creek where they broke ranks. These encounters frequently resulted in bloody noses and broken bones. If the South gained, the trophies were taken to the Common. If the victory fell to the North, to Copp's Hill, where they were burned.

1766. FEBRUARY 14.

The Liberty Tree on Essex Street was pruned.

APRIL 21.

Two fire engines went to guard the Power House on the Common.

MAY 16.

The news of the "Repeal of the Stamp Act" by Parliament, caused universal acclamation. At a meeting in Faneuil Hall, the 19th was appointed for public rejoicing. The day was ushered in by the ringing of bells and the roar of cannon. Flags waved from the houses and the shipping in the harbor with martial music. Captain Paddock's Artillery fired a salute, amid great hurrahs, on the Common. Across the way the residence of Mr. Hancock—where a grand entertainment was going on—was lighted up, (and) shone through the trees. A pipe of Madeira was given to outsiders. A pyramid, on the Common, lighted by 280 lamps, displayed patriotic paintings, and a grand exhibition of fireworks closed the evening. Illuminations shone and bonfires blazed in all parts of the town.

MAY 19.

The Repeal of the Stamp Act passed in 1765 caused a grand celebration on the Common. The *Boston Post* Boy, of the 26th, says: "Friday se—tonight to the Inexpressible Joy of all we received, by Captain Coffin, the important News of the Repeal of the Stamp Act which was signed by His Majesty on the 18th of March last. In the Evening the whole Town was beautifully illuminated. On the Common the Sons of Liberty erected a magnificent Pyramid illuminated with 28 Lamps; the four upper stories of which were ornamented with Figures of their Majesties, and fourteen of the worthy Patriots who have distinguished themselves in their Love of Liberty. On the Top of the Pyramid was fixed a round Box of Fireworks horizontally. About 100 yards from the Pyramid the Sons of Liberty erected a Stage for the Exhibition of their Fireworks, near the Work House, in the lower Room of which they entertained the Gentlemen of the Town. John Hancock, Esq., who gave a grand and elegant Entertainment to the genteel Part of the Town, and treated the Populace with a Pipe of Madeira Wine, erected at the Front of his House, which was magnificently illuminated, a Stage for the Exhibition of his Fireworks, which was to answer those of the Sons of Liberty. At Dusk the Scene opened by the Discharge of twelve Rockets from each Stage, after which the Figures on the Pyramid were uncovered, making a beautiful Appearance. To give a description of the great beauty of Fireworks exhibited from this Time till Eleven o'clock would be endless—the Air was filled with Rockets—the Ground with Bee-hives and Serpents—and the two Stages with Wheels of Fireworks of various sorts......At Eleven o'clock the signal being given by a Discharge of 21 Rockets, the horizontal Wheel on the Top of the Pyramid or Obelisk was played off, ending in the Discharge of sixteen Dozen of Serpents in the Air, which concluded the Show......The Pyramid, which was designed to be placed under the Tree of Liberty, as a standing Monument of this glorious Aera, by accident took Fire about One o'clock, and was consumed."

May 19.

One of the Features of the celebration of the Repeal of the Stamp Act was an Obelisk, with allegorical figures;—one representing "American in Distress"—all lighted by 280 lamps, being erected on the Common. It was burned in the celebration.

May 19.

John Rowe, a Boston merchant, in expressing the joy on the Repeal of the Stamp Act, writes in his "diary"—"Mr. Hancock behaved very well on this occasion & treated every Person with Cheerfulness. I contributed as much to General joy as Any Person. The whole was much admired & the day Crowned with Glory & honour."

May 20.

The Liberty Tree was lighted with 108 lanterns at night, 45 shone the previous evening, showing the majority that repealed the act.

John G. Hales, "Surveyor and Typographer" printed a "Survey of Boston and its vicinity" which contains a Table showing the rate, per hour, a person is moving by the time taken to pass the long Mall from the fence on Park Street to the fence on Boylston Street, "Passing through the Mall," as shown by the first twenty entries, was done in 19 minutes, 8-86 seconds. And a score ten miles an hour is found when the Mall is walked in 1 minute, 54.85 seconds.

The 29th Regiment encamped on the Common.

1767 October 25.

The eighth anniversary of the reign of King George, 12 o'clock, a Royal salute was fired from the Castle which was followed by three volleys from the Regiment drawn upon the Common.

NOVEMBER 20.

New revenue laws went into effect. A hand bill was posted under the Liberty Tree when Bernard wrote: "Under the tree was stuck up a paper so highly seditious, that it would be undoubtedly deemed in England an overt act of high treason. It contained an exhortation to the Sons of Liberty to rise on that day, and fight for their rights; stating "that if they assembled, they would be joined by legions; that, if they neglected this opportunity, they would be cursed by all posterity."

A hospital, not intended for infectious diseases, was established near the foot of the Common.

1768 MARCH 18.

Effigies of Commissioner Paxton and Inspector Williams were suspended from Liberty Tree. A festive company met at the British Coffee House where a toast drank was "The Boston Gazette." The town was quiet though, it was said, that, the British Commissioners would be obliged "to resign their commissions" under Liberty Tree.

JUNE 4.

The birthday of George III was celebrated, for the last time in Boston, when many went to the Common.

JUNE 10.

The Liberty—a sloop of war—owned by John Hancock, lay loaded with wine at Hancock's wharf at night. The wine was taken out without any entry at the Custom House. It was resolved to seize the sloop! the seizure was made just at an hour when the working classes were returning home, so a large crowd gathered on the wharf. The sloop was removed down under the guns of the Romney, but the mob, which had now grown to immense proportions, and who not understanding all the circumstances, became furious; stones and missiles were thrown at the Collector Joseph Harrison and the Comptroller Benjamin Hallowell. One of the inspectors was beaten by clubs and sticks and had his sword broken. Richard Aclom Harrison, a son of the Collector—who accompanied his father, was thrown down, dragged by the hair, and otherwise badly bruised, while the Collector's elegant pleasure boat was dragged to the Common and burned.

June 10.

Bernard says: that "the riot was followed by papers, stuck upon Liberty Tree, containing an invitation to rise, and clear the country of the Commissioners and their officers.

June 14.

A town meeting, to restore order, was called under Liberty Tree. A flag waved from the tree.

July 8.

A schooner, loaded with molasses, lying at the wharf at night, was seized for violating customs laws, and was held by two officers when thirty men went aboard, and, placing the officers in the cabin carted off the cargo which was restored by the Selectmen. Governor Bernard now wrote: "So we are not without a government, only it is in the hands of the people of the Town, and not of those deputed by the King, or under his authority." The affair of the "Liberty" with the Riot had now been heard of by the Ministry who ordered two Regiments to sail from Ireland to Boston and also troops from Halifax. Apprehensions were felt that the arrival of the troops might cause trouble, so that at a Town Convention held September 15th it was requested that the inhabitants should "provide themselves with firearms, that they may be prepared in case of sudden danger." A Fast Day was also appointed though but few were aware of the alarm that pervaded the minds of the people. It was rumored abroad that 10,000 armed men would resist the arrival of the English soldiers. Groups assembled on the Common.

SEPTEMBER 10.

A tar barrel, intended to be fired in case any British troops arrived in town, was placed in the skillet of the Beacon. This was thought to be an insult to the Governor (Bernard) so it was stealthily taken down.

SEPTEMBER 30.

Twelve vessels, entered the harbor and anchored in the N. E. part of the Town, and the next day the troops landed on Long Wharf, and "with drums beating and fifes playing" marched into King Street and thence to the Common where the 29th Regiment was encamped, the 14th Regiment finding shelter in Faneuil Hall, other troops occupying the State House, which was considered an insult to the Town and the Colony. A picture by Paul Revere copied from "Edes and Gills, North American Almanack and Massachusetts Register for the year 1770" clearly represents the "Prospective View of the Town of Boston, the Capitol of New England; and the Landing of the Troops, in the year 1768."

OCTOBER 1.

A threat had long been made to overawe the inhabitants when a British fleet anchored in the harbor having on board the 14th and 29th Regiments, a portion of the 59th with a train of artillery, all under command of Lieutenant-Colonel Dalrymple, landing at Long Wharf proceeded along King Street and to the Common. A profound silence existed among the "Sons of Liberty." As Governor Bernard had gone to Jamaica Plain the soldiers returned to the fleet.

OCTOBER 29.

The 29th Regiment left the Common finding new quarters in the house of Mayor Green, a distiller, in Green's Lane, and in the house of Mr. Forrest in New Boston.

OCTOBER 31.

Richard Ames, a deserter, was shot, on the Common, and buried on the same spot. The affair was thought to be one of unjust severity, it not being a time of war, and some ladies, prominent in the Town, tried, though vainly, to secure his pardon from the commanding-general.

NOVEMBER 10.

The *News-Letter* says: "Several transports arrived here this morning, from Cork, having on board part of the 64th and 65th Regiments, the remainder are not yet in." These troops were quartered in the Castle on the Common. Boston had now changed into a garrisoned town. The Common was covered with white tents.

The Beacon Light fell by some unknown cause.

A gate near the Granary was closed "except for the carrying in, or bringing out, powder for the magazine."

Paul Revere's engraving shows buildings along the shore but none on Beacon Hill.

Adams, Warren and Hancock, whose portraits hang in Faneuil Hall, were seen walking on the Common.

1769. MARCH 13.

A committee was appointed by the Selectmen, "to consider what measures may be proper to be taken for the preservation of the Common, and preventing any incumbrances being laid thereon, to inquire into the title of the lands" and to report, "as soon as may be." This movement was, probably, suggested by the late occupation of the Common by the soldiering. It was also voted "not to rent the land, on which the gun house is erected, to the officers of the train of Artillery of the Regiment of the Town," while among the reported grievances was horse racing on the Common by members of the army.

JULY 17.

The *Boston Gazette* advertises a small Red Cow "strayed away from the Common. . . . . Whosoever hath or shall stop said Cow, are desired to inform the Printers hereof, and they shall be Rewarded for their Trouble."

JULY 31.

Governor Bernard sailed from Boston to return to England. Salutes were fired from Hancock's Wharf and a flag waved from Liberty Tree. Bonfires shone on the hills at night.

Sheriff Greenleaf was ordered, by the Court, to "cause a new gallows to be erected on the Neck, the old one having gone to decay."

A Regimental Hospital was established at the foot of the Common.

A hospital at the foot of the Common, took fire and was partially destroyed.

1770 JANUARY 13.

The Boston Massacre arose from a riot caused by the British soldiers being hooted by men and boys who had the sympathies of the inhabitants. A number of fights occurred with straggling soldiers when finally a picket guard, composed of eight men, were unable to bear further insults. A brawl broke out in an alley when some Brattle Street soldiers rushed into King Street, and, brandishing their arms, yelled, "Where are the cowards! Where are the scoundrels!" and fired into a crowd killing three and badly wounding five persons. The "Old Brick Church" bell rung and the town was thrown into great excitement as the inhabitants rushed out, armed with sticks and stones taken from the market, filling the streets at midnight. A cry of fire was raised when some engines rushed to the scene. "The soldiers are rising," was the cry, and only by great precautions was a general outbreak averted. The next morning a meeting was held in Faneuil Hall, and, in the afternoon, citizens again met in the "Old South Meeting house,—the largest building in the town—

when it was resolved "that nothing could be expected to restore peace, and prevent blood and carnage, but the immediate removal of the troops." Not a soldier was ever again seen outside of the Common, or barracks, on the streets after dark. Mr. Adams, said a "Motley mob of saucy boys, negroes and mulattoes, Irish teagues, and outlandish Jack-tars." The funeral of the victims of the "Boston Massacre" was attended by a vast concourse of people, amid great pomp and ceremony, at the Granary Burying Ground.

FEBRUARY 22.

The arrival of tea vessels in Boston Harbor created a widespread indignation and one of the results was the sad shooting of a German boy named Snyder, eleven years old. A pole, with a figure on the head, was erected near the store of a man named Lilly, which had drawn a crowd of boys at night. A man named Richardson, a custom sympathizer, who had failed to remove the pole, was hooted by the boys, and who, ran into the house and fired a shot into the crowd fatally wounding Snyder. The *Boston Gazette*, says, "The untimely death of this amiable youth will be a standing monument to posterity, that the time was when innocence itself was not safe." The body of young Snyder was placed under the Liberty Tree—on the Common—and seen by great crowds, when it was followed by four, or five hundred school boys, marching in couples to the grave.

MARCH 5.

The arrival of the British troops in Boston gave rise to much excitement. At nine o'clock in the evening fire bells called the people together in King Street.

Captain Preston, who commanded the main guard, was "told that it was a plan of the people to massacre the soldiers and that a tar-barrel was to be fired on Beacon Hill to bring in the people from the country." No bloodshed ensued.

MARCH 8.

The funeral of the four victims of the Boston Massacre—Samuel Gray, James Caldwell, Crispus Attucks, and Samuel Maverick—took place. A long train of carriages was followed by prominent citizens while the bells tolled in Boston, and the adjoining towns, as the procession proceeded to the Granary Burying Ground.

MARCH 14.

Another victim of the Massacre—Patrick Carr, who was shot, was buried from Faneuil Hall and laid in the vault with the other victims in the middle of the Granary Burying Ground.

LAST WEDNESDAY IN MAY.

The annual election of the King's Council, by the General Court, took place at Cambridge when the election sermon was preached by Rev. Samuel Cooke. The "Friends of the liberties of North America" caused great crowds to gather on the streets of Boston and on the Common. Rev. Dr. Chauncy preached from the text: "Our fathers trusted in thee; they trusted, and thou didst deliver them." There was also "an elegant Entertainment" at Faneuil Hall, where between five and six hundred gentlemen assembled and which, it was said, was "attended with that cheerfulness, Decency and good Order Peculiar to the Favorites of Freedom and Science." The *Boston Gazette and Country Journal,* Monday, June 4th, says, "The Morning was ushered in with Musick, parading the streets, and an Ox which on the afternoon before was conveyed thro' the Town decorated with Ribbons, Flowers, etc. was early put to the Fire at the Bottom of the Common; the Novelty of an Ox roasting whole, excited the Curiosity of the People, and incredible Numbers from this and the neighboring Towns resorted to the Spot, to view so unusual a Spectacle."

Two Malls; the Great Mall and the Little Mall—the former bordering the east side of the Common and the latter the east side of the Granary Burying Ground. Colonel Paddock had planted English elms on the Little Mall. The Great Mall was grown with elms and button woods for half a century.

Sunrise and sunset guns were fired from Beacon Hill.

1771

The title of the Common was carefully searched when a Committee of Selectmen was appointed to "inclose the Common agreeable to order of the Town."

John Hancock, a public spirited Townsman, had a stand erected where a band gave concerts each pleasant afternoon.

The Common, the popular resort, was beautified by more Trees with Walks and Malls.

1772 MAY.

Criminals, with ropes around their necks, sit on the gallows on the Neck.

JUNE.

From a Newspaper—"A young man of about twenty years of age, from the country, mounted on a stage, in the Common, and preached from the words, "If the righteous scarcely are saved, where shall the ungodly and sinner appear!" The audience which consisted of about twenty persons when the service began had increased to several thousand at the close.

1773 JANUARY.

Independence began to be talked of in Boston and on the Common.

OCTOBER 21.

Lewis Ames was hung, on the Common, for robbery.

NOVEMBER 3.

A hand bill, posted around, called the Freemen of Boston, and the neighboring towns, to assemble at Liberty Tree to witness the resignations and the oath of allegiance of the consignees who avowed to reship any tea that should arrive in port. A flag floated from the top of Liberty Tree, the town crier walked through the streets summoning the people, and the town bells rang from eleven to twelve o'clock. Adams, Hancock and Phillips were present and the character, intelligence and wealth of the inhabitants were represented by many prominent people.

NOVEMBER 3.

Three well known consignees were asked to meet under the Liberty Tree and resign their commission as consignees of the East India Company's tea. Several hundred persons met on the Common, though the consignees did not appear. A committee was appointed and a town meeting held. John Hancock, presiding. The consignees refused to resign, and when the news came that the tea ships had sailed for Boston the House of one Clarke was surrounded by a hooting, howling, mob and a pistol fired at one of the windows. A large public meeting was held at Faneuil Hall where feelings of high indignation arose and tea denounced as a pernicious weed." When the three vessels arrived no clearance was permitted and the anticipated storm broke forth in great fury. A band of fifty men disguised as Indians, "very dark complexioned persons, dressed like Mohawks, of very grotesque appearance," went to Faneuil Hall, and giving a loud "war whoop," were haranged by Josiah Quincy who urged the need of adhering to the sentiments of the people. The band then proceeded to the wharf, and, at dusk, while an anxious crowd looked on, boarded the vessels throwing 342 chests into the water. A portion of a chest, that had been sold, was seized and the money forfeited, when it was carried, by a triumphant procession, and burned before the house of Mr. Hancock, who stood, smilingly, in the doorway. The event was celebrated by bonfires on the Common.

NOVEMBER 3.

A meeting was called to protest against importing the East India Company's tea. Several hundred persons assembled under the Liberty Tree, at noon, when a Committee was appointed to wait upon the consignees, but who refused to listen to them.

1774 JUNE 28.

Thomas Jefferson had a reception in Boston and visited the Common.

JUNE.

On a Thursday and Saturday three transports, filled with troops arrived in Kings Road and the harbor, and the following Monday landed on Long Wharf. On board was His Majesty's 4th Regiment which, landing on Monday, marched up to the Common. On Saturday the other transport arrived with the 42nd Regiment on board which also encamped on the Common. Two others were daily expected from Ireland, a part of them arriving the next week.

AUGUST 8.

The house of Earl Percy, built early in the century, stood opposite the Common where many guests passed in and out the door. Each afternoon the Earl was seen crossing the Common within a stone's throw of the camp.

AUGUST 10.

Four delegates—Thomas Cushing, Robert Treat Paine, Samuel and John Adams—on leaving Boston were drawn in a coach preceded by two white servants, who rode armed, with four colored servants behind—two mounted on horses and two afoot. They passed five regiments encamped in tents on the Common.

AUGUST.

The Fusiliers arrived and encamped on Fort Hill and also a force from Halifax. Barracks were now built on the Common. At the close of the year General Gage had eleven regiments under his command, besides several companies of artillery and a naval force.

SEPTEMBER 1.

Valentine Ducat was shot, on the Common, for desertion.

SEPTEMBER 27.

Soldiers practiced on a target placed in the stream at the foot of the Common.

DECEMBER 24.

William Ferguson was shot on the Common for desertion.

SATURDAY, DECEMBER 24.

The diary of a British Officer (said to be Lieutenant John Barker, of the Fourth King's Own Regiment of Foot) contains the following: "Bad day; constant snow 'till evening, when it turned out rain and sleet. A soldier of the Tenth shot for desertion; the only thing done in remembrance of Christmas Day." A gloomy holiday.

Boston—the Puritan town—was greatly indignant that the British soldiers raced their horses on the Common, on Sundays, or disturbed church services by playing Yankee Doodle outside the church doors.

The Town and Common—at this time, are vividly described by Dr. Holmes:

"The streets are thronged with trampling feet,
The northern hill is ridged with graves,
But night and morn the drum is beat
To frighten down the "rebel knaves."
The stones of King Street still are red,
And yet the bloody red-coats come;

I hear their pacing sentry's tread,
The click of steel, the tap of drum,
And over all the open green,
Where grazed of late the harmless kine,
The cannon's deepening ruts are seen,
The war-horse stamps, the bayonets shine."

REVOLUTIONARY PERIOD

1775 MARCH.

The fence before Hancock's House, opposite the Common, was cut and defaced by drunken British officers so that it was necessary to apply for a guard.

APRIL 18.

Percy's brigade slept all night on the Common. A walk (now) from Providence Station to West Street covers the line of encampment where rings in the grass long showed where the white tents stood.

APRIL 18.

The Young Folks History of the United States, by Colonel Thomas Wentworth Higginson, (1875), says: "The patriots kept close watch at Charlestown agreeing that if any large force of troops were ordered out by night in Boston, a lantern should be hung from the North Church. One night the watchers on the Charlestown side of Charles River saw the lantern gleaming in the steeple. Instantly all were in motion." Paul Revere's ride is described thus: "So he galloped on from house to house, awakening all the principal farmers; and we may well suppose that there was no more sleep in any house that night after Paul Revere had passed by......Meantime some 800 British soldiers, embarking in boats at the foot of Boston Common crossed to what is now East Cambridge. They marched silently along the marshes; when suddenly the bells of the country towns began to ring and it was plain that the alarm had been given."

April 19.

Earl Percy's Brigade formed along the Mall and started for Lexington.

April 19.

The "First blow for liberty" was struck when, on this night, at ten o'clock, the King's Troops started out from the bottom of the Common for Lexington. Crossing over Phip's farm they proceeded as far as Concord, destroying Magazines, Provisions, and spiking some cannon. The patriots warned by Paul Revere who had been signalled by the lanterns hung from the steeple of the North Church—"one by sea, two by land" rushed out of their homes. During the retreat the British joined by Lord Percy's brigade, were harassed, from the trees and bushes, and all the way to Charlestown, until sunset. Thirty patriots were killed and fifty of the King's troops.

April 19.

Between one and two o'clock in the morning the inhabitants of Boston were startled by the ringing of a bell. Eight hundred British left the foot of the Common, and, embarking in boats and barges, crossed to Cambridge and reached Lexington Meeting house just before sunrise.

April 19.

Lord Percy's troops formed for the relief of the retreating British from Concord. The line extended from Scollay's Square to the Common.

MAY 17.

A disastrous fire occurred in Boston caused by some soldiers handling cartridges, which, exploding, set fire to a store used as a barrack. The flames, spreading quickly, destroyed thirty warehouses and buildings. Many donations of food and clothing, sent to the poor of Boston were consumed and great confusion prevailed as the fire engines were worked by the soldiers, who, not understanding how to work them, were obliged to call the citizens. No bells were rung, but the alarm was sounded by the "taps o'er drum" which caused a rumor that the Whigs had set fire to the town. Much excitement prevailed on the Common.

AUGUST.

The liberty tree was cut down by the British soldiers on the Common, when a soldier was killed by falling from a limb. The *Essex Gazette* (31st) says, "Armed with axes, they made a furious attack upon it. After a long spell of laughing and grinning, sweating, swearing, and foaming, with malice diabolical, they cut down a tree because it bore the name of liberty."

SEPTEMBER 22.

At twelve o'clock volleys were fired on the Common, Bunker Hill, the Ships in the harbor and the Castle, in honor of the king.

OCTOBER.

The Continental troops, outside the town, made frequent attacks on the British camp on the Common.

One man wrote that "our boats went up within gunshot of the Common, and, alarmed by firing, and then returned without any loss on our side." Dr. Belknap says, "that two floating batteries came within three-quarters of a mile of the botton of the Common, and that the shot fired from that point" struck the tents on the Common, and killed one man, and the manufactory house which is an hospital, which occasioned the removal of the sick, also the Lamb Tavern and Martin Brimmer House."

Some men from Cambridge sailed by Brookline Fort, down the Bay, and, approaching near the Common, opened fire on the town.

S. A. Drake, in the "Landmarks of Boston," says: "The position of the British defences and encampments on the Common, during the winter of 1775-6, were as follows: A small earthwork was thrown up at the northwest corner, a little higher up than the present entrance on Charles Street; this was designed for infantry, and held by a single company. The little elevation mentioned by the name of Fox Hill (near the present "Centre Gate" of the Public Garden on Charles Street) was nearly or quite surrounded by water at times, and was hence called the island; on this was a small redoubt. At the southwest corner, at a point at high water mark, now intersected by Boylston Street extension, was another breastwork for infantry...... On the westerly slope of the hill, overlooking the parade, on which the flagstaff is now situated, was a square redoubt, behind which lay encamped a battalion of infantry; to the east, and on a line with the eastern-most point of the hill, were two half-moons for small arms, with a second battalion in its rear. About opposite Carver Street, resting on the southwest corner of the burial ground, was a bastioned work, directly across Boylston Street. This was the second line. On the hill formerly known as Flagstaff Hill, but now dedicated to the soldiers' monument, the artillery was posted, protected by intrenchments.

Immediately behind this hill, stretching from the burial ground across to Beacon Street Mall were the camps of three battalions of infantry. . . . . . None of the works were formidable except the most southern, which was connected with the line on the Neck.

The Common was an intrenched camp, with a regular garrison of 1750 men."

The familiar story may be retold of the Boston boys whose snow slides had been destroyed by British soldiers, and, who, finding no redress went to General Gage, who said "What! have your fathers been teaching you rebellion, and sent you here to exhibit it?" To which one of the boys replied, "Nobody sent us, sir. We have never injured, nor insulted your troops; but they have been spoiling our snow-slides, so that we cannot use them any more. We complained; and they called us 'Young rebels,' and told us to help ourselves if we could. We told the Captain this; and they laughed at us. Yesterday our slides were destroyed once more; and we will bear it no longer!" The General, who could not but admire their "love of liberty in the air they breathed," assured them that their snow-slides should not be interfered with any more.

The British army now occupied all the grounds on the west side of the Common from Beacon Hill to the sea, and the pastures on the west side of Pleasant Street.

The British fortified all the highest points of the town, including Beacon, Powder House and Fox Hills.

A fort was built on West Hill and a strong barricade on the Common.

The British went through their manoeuvres, on the Common, Sundays and week days.

One British, writes: "There was a number of our men went a scating on the Bay, near Boston Common, and the enemy fired upwards of a hundred small arms that did no damage."

The Common was occupied and fortified by 1700 British soldiers until the evacuation of Boston. A redoubt was built on Flagstaff Hill and the Powder House stood near the Frog Pond, while trenches were dug all along the Back Bay. It was thought Washington intended to attack the town.

Small-pox, dysentery, scurvy, and other ailments led to a large mortality among the British soldiers who were buried in trenches at the foot of the Common.

The wooden fence, around the Common, was demolished and used for fuel by the British soldiers.

Several of the largest trees on the Mall were cut down by the vandalism of the British soldiers, while cellars and ditches dug throughout the camp greatly disfigured the Common and of which traces were visible long after the evacuation.

General Gage issued a proclamation when a Tory wrote some doggerel lines closing with the following:

"And now my song is at an end,
And to conclude my ditty,
It is the poor and ignorant,
And only them I pity.
As for their king, John Hancock,
And Adams, the're taken

Their hearts for signs shall hang up high
Upon that hill call'd Beacon!"

The Ancient and Honorable Artillery Company were forbidden to parade on the Common.

Prayers were held on the Common.

1776 JANUARY.

During the occupation of Boston, by the British, assemblies and dances, disapproved by the residents, were held at Concert Hall, on the southerly corner of Court and Hanover Streets, (8th). The "Blockade of Boston" was performed at Fanueil Hall, which was altered into a theatre, where Washington was caricatured wearing a wig, and with a rusty sword, standing beside a squire holding a rusty gun. The tragedy of "Zara" was also given.

The following was the programme:

ON SATURDAY NEXT
WILL BE PERFORMED BY A SOCIETY OF
LADIES AND GENTLEMEN AT FANEUIL HALL
THE TRAGEDY OF ZARA.

The expenses of the House being paid, the overplus will be apply'd to the Benefit of the Widows and Children of the soldiers. No money will be taken at the Door, but Tickets will be delivered Today and Tomorrow, between the hours of Eight and Two, at Doctor Morris's in School Street.

Pit, One Dollar Gallery, Quarter of a Dollar

The Doors to be open at Five, and begin precisely at six o'clock.

***Tickets for Friday will be taken.

Vivant Rex et Regina.

The evening had a serious turn when, during one of the acts, a Sergeant rushed on the stage shouting "The Yankees are attacking our works at Bunker Hill!" Everyone thought it a part of the play, but when General Howe, who was present, gave the order, "Officers, to your alarm posts!" a panic ensued and the entire audience rushed to the doors. Women fainted and shrieked. Major Knowlton had made a raid on Charlestown Neck where he had set fire to some houses, used by the British, killing one man and taking five prisoners. The conflagration, seen in Boston had caused the excitement.

These performances were attended by soldiers stationed on the Common.

SUNDAY, MARCH 17.

When the British evacuated Boston the Americans occupied the town, at two o'clock p. m., a party from Cambridge landing on the Common.

MARCH 17.

Flags were waved, amid public congratulations, on the evacuation, by the British, of Boston and the Common.

SPRING.

The body of Major General Joseph Warren, killed at Bunker Hill, preceded by several Freemason lodges and followed by thousands of his fellow citizens, was carried from the spot where he fell to King's Chapel where religious services were held when the remains were buried in the "Minot Tomb" in the Granary Burying Ground.

SEPTEMBER 19.

The pole on Beacon Hill was again raised.

When Washington occupied Dorchester Heights it was ordered as a part of the plan, in case of an attack from the British General Howe, General Putnam, with two divisions, should assault the works on Beacon Hill. Had the expected attack been made the Common would have been the scene of a battle of the Revolution adding to its historic charm.

1777 OCTOBER 5.

Elijah Woodward was shot, on the Common, for desertion.

The "Massachusetts State Train," an artillery Regiment, raised for the defense of Boston, figured prominently. Colonel Thomas Crafts issued an order directing Captain Stoddard and Lieutenant Hinkley to hold their detachments in readiness to "embarque" for Dorchester, and then, with arms and accoutrements, to proceed by land to Boston and assemble on the Common.

1778 JANUARY 7.

The arrival of the Hon. John Hancock was announced by the ringing of bells and the firing of Cannon by Colonel Crafts artillery on the Common.

SEPTEMBER 19.

A circus opened at the foot of the Mall.

There were many old nooks and corners, taverns and inns, coffee-houses, loitering places for news and gossip, also resorts where boys and negroes met for play and roguery, on wharf, or lane, were dark holes of ill repute, all of whose frequenters were seen on the Common.

1779 JUNE 1.

When Admiral DeEstaing visited Boston a reception was given to him at the Hancock mansion when the Common, it was said, was "bedizened with lace" as the officers walked up Beacon Hill. The cows were all milked.

NATIONAL PERIOD

1780 — MAY 19.

A dark day, caused by smoke from the burning of trees in the Maine woods, frightened many people in town and on the Common.

SEPTEMBER 10.

Counterfeiters, with ropes about their necks, were placed on the gallows on the Neck.

A gentleman named Willard, while making observations, on the Common, was suddenly approached by a stranger who, running through the crowd, breathlessly, exclaimed, "The tide has ceased to flow!" "So it has for today," replied Mr. W. taking out his watch, *" 'tis past twelve o'clock."*

The Common originally extended as far as Mason Street and the whole block of houses—Colonnade Row—was built upon it, though its dimensions were enlarged by the town purchasing about two acres of ground, belonging to William Foster, on Boylston Street, east of the burying ground and extending as far as Tremont Street.

The "Pendulum Ferry boat" ran from the foot of the Common across to Charlestown.

1781 OCTOBER 17.

The surrender of Cornwallis on this date was subsequently celebrated by a large bonfire with great crowds on the Common.

The principal taverns were the White Horse, the Black Horse, the Lamb, and the Oliver Cromwell, kept by a man named Brackett, in School Street. Then there were four public houses; the oldest was the Admiral Vernon at the lower corner of Merchants Row, the Bunch of Grapes was kept by Colonel Marston at the corner of Kilby Street, the Coffee House, by Deacon Jones, on the site of the Massachusetts Bank, and the fourth kept by Mr. Gray, at the corner of Royal Exchange Lane and called the Exchange. Many lodgers sat on the Common.

1782 JUNE.

The birth of the Dauphin was celebrated in Boston and "a number of rockets, wheels, bee-hives and other fireworks displayed on the Common."

1783 MAY 23.

James Otis—Revolutionary patriot—was killed by a stroke of lightning while "leaning upon his cane at the front door" of the house of his friend, Isaac Osgood at Andover, Massachusetts, and was buried in the Granary Burying Ground the following Monday; the body was preceded to the grave by the "Honorable Fraternity of Free and Accepted Masons" and followed by a long train of citizens.

July 4.

The first oration was delivered by Dr. John Warren. Fireworks were seen on the Common.

It was a matter of gratification that the trees, on the Common, were not injured during the Revolution.

It was ordered that the part of the Common between the Granary and the North end be places for the Wood Markets for the sale of all the wood brought into the town.

1784 January 1.

A liberty pole was raised on the spot of the Liberty Tree.

March 4.

Terms of peace being definitely settled between England and the Colonies a day of celebration was appointed, which, says the *Continental Journal and Weekly Advertiser,* "was ushered in with the ringing of bells and discharge of cannon which continued, by intervals, throughout the day......The Governor's House, with the public buildings, was beautifully illuminated and, at seven o'clock, a grand exhibition of fireworks was displayed, on the Common, such as were never before equalled in this place.

October 28.

Grant and Cover were hung, on the Common, for murder.

Blackstone's spring ran in crystal brightness until

the opening of Louisburg Square, covering a period of half a century.

The Common was greatly improved by private subscription, "low portions were raised, holes filled up, uneven places graded, fences repaired and trees planted."

A wooden fence, around the Common, used by the British for fuel was replaced by a subscription started by Dr. Oliver Smith.

A third row of trees was planted by Oliver Smith and others, inside the two rows on the Common.

A third row of trees was planted on the Tremont Street Mall.

A third row of trees was planted, near the Mall, on the Common.

CONFEDERATION PERIOD

1785 MAY 5.

William Scott and Thomas Archibald were hung, on the Common, for committing burglary.

A Musick Gallery, kept by Mr. Eaton, stood near the Mall.

The Columbian Museum, with a wax works exhibition, was at the head of the Common.

The Pantheon (a riding school) was at the foot of the Mall.

Foot races on the Charles Street Mall.

There seemed, apparently to be an indiscriminate use of both Mall and Common.

An "Onlooker" writes in the Massachusetts Centinel, "In the evening very few were in the Mall, though we fear some were disappointed of their customary tour to that frequented place, upon account of a severe gust of wind. That many of the fair were detained from principle and not the weather we are induced to believe is the cause, and that the happiness of our females is built upon a foundation more permanent than wind.

We, however, commiserate the disappointment of some and with the next Sunday may afford some gentler relaxation from divine service."

1786 JANUARY 6.

An earthquake, which did considerable damage in town, was felt on the Common.

NOVEMBER 9.

A severe earthquake, which lasted for three minutes, was felt on the Common.

Governor Hancock, Governor Bowdoin, Thomas Russell, Esq., and others raised a sum to improve the Common. Trees were planted on Park Street.

1787 MAY 23.

It was voted that "the Selectmen allot for the Light Horse the west part of the Common to the beach for exercising horses."

JUNE.

An attempt was made to remove the State House from the Common.

NOVEMBER 22.

John Sheehan, a native of Cork, Ireland, was executed, on the Common, for committing a burglary in the house of Mr. T. Elliot on the previous June. His behavior at the last was calm and he met his end with composure. He was a Roman Catholic, twenty-four years old. The *Centinel* says, "except for the burglary for which he suffered, (he) does not appear, by his life, to have been guilty of many atrocious offences."

Two acres and an eighth, belonging to William Foster, in the south corner and extending as far as the burying ground, became a part of the Common.

The portion occupied by the Deer Park including Park Street, became a part of the Common.

A Gunhouse, Hay scales and School-house stood on the Common.

Boys threw balls up against Beacon Hill catching them as they rebounded.

1788 JANUARY 19.

Lieutenant Governor Thomas Cushing died, aged 63, and was buried in the Granary burying ground. Inscription: "He took an active part in the Revolutionary conflict and was several years Speaker of the House of Representatives of Massachusetts, until he became a member of the Continental Congress in the year 1774-5."

MAY 8.

Archibald Taylor and Joseph Taylor were hung, on the Neck, for robbing a Mr. Cunningham. The robbery was committed near the spot of execution.

The Frog Pond was a small mud hole on the Common.

1789 JULY.

The *Massachusetts Magazine* contained a "View of the Seat of His Excellency John Hancock, Esq., Boston," by Hill.

OCTOBER 8.

William Dannesse, William Smith and Rachel Wall were all hung, on the Common, for highway robbery.

OCTOBER 24.

General Washington visited Boston when much excitement prevailed throughout the town and on the Common.

Massachusetts adopted the Constitution when the Convention dined and drank toasts. A grand procession walked the streets with representations of agriculture, the trades, the ship "Federal Constitution," drawn by thirteen horses, with a crew of thirteen men, Captain, Seamen and Militia companies. Salutes were fired in front of the State House when a grand dinner ended the day's proceedings. In the evening another procession drew the boat "The Old Constitution" to the Common where amid loud hurrahs, it was burned.

The Beacon was blown down.

1790 MAY.

A monument, commemorating the patriots who fell at Bunker Hill, 60 feet in height and enclosed by a fence with seats for visitors, affording a charming view of the town, bay and surrounding country, was completed on Beacon Hill. Four tablets which are preserved in Doric Hall in the State House,—are inscribed as follows:

Tablet on the South Side.

"To commemorate that train of events which led to the American Revolution and finally secured Liberty and Independence to the United States. This column is erected by the voluntary contributions of the citizens of Boston, MDCCXC."

Tablet on the North Side.

"Stamp Act passed 1765, Repealed 1766.

Board of Customs established 1767.

British troops fired on the Inhabitants of Boston, March 5, 1770. Tea Act passed 1773. Tea destroyed in Boston Decem 16. Port of Boston shut and guarded June 1, 1774.

General Congress at Philadelphia, Septem 14. Provincial Congress at Concord Oct. 11. Battle of Lexington April 19, 1775. Battle of Bunker Hill, June 17. Washington took command of the Army, July 2. Boston Evacuated, March 17, 1776. Independence Declared by Congress, July 4, 1776. Hancock President."

Tablet on the West Side.

"Capture of Hessians at Trenton, Dec. 26th, 1776. Capture of Hessians at Bennington, Aug. 16, 1777. Capture of British Army at Saratoga, Oct. 17. Alliance with France, Feb. 6, 1778. Confederation of the United States formed July 9. Constitution of Massachusetts formed 1780. Bowdoin President of Convention. Capture of British Army at York, Oct. 19, 1781. Preliminaries of Peace, Nov. 30, 1782. Definitive Treaty of Peace, Sep. 10, 1783. Federal Constitution formed Sep. 17, 1787, and ratified by the United States, 1787-1790. New Congress Assembled at New

York, April 6, 1780. Washington Inaugurated President, April 30. Public Debts funded, Aug. 4, 1790."

Tablet on the East Side.

"Americans, while from this eminence scenes of luxuriant fertility, of flourishing commerce and the abodes of social happiness meet your view, forget not those who, by their exertions, have secured to you these blessings."

JULY 4.

The children of the Almshouse, on the Common, were dined by Governor Hancock.

OCTOBER 14.

Edward Vail (white) and John Bailey (colored) were hung, on the Common, for burglary.

NOVEMBER 6.

Governor James Bowdoin died, in Boston and was buried in the Granary Burying Ground when "Captain Johnson's Artillery was paraded on Beacon Hill and discharged minute guns during the solemnities." His name is honored in Bowdoin College.

Rev. Jesse Lee, a Methodist, preached under the Great Elm, on the Common, to larger crowds than any since Whitefield.

Boston was a thriving town with its windmills, Meeting Houses, Sloops tied to the docks, Market Place, Stately Mansions, Gloomy Prison, Old Taverns whose quaint signs hung outside, Whipping Post, Beacon and the Common.

1791 MAY 16.

An earthquake, doing considerable damage in town, was felt on the Common.

1792 FEBRUARY 22.

Washington's birthday was celebrated in Boston when many walked on the Common.

SEPTEMBER 4.

Nathaniel Cutting, on a visit to Boston, alluding to the obelisk on Beacon Hill, said it reminded one of "a farthing candle placed in a large candle-stick upon the altar of some Roman Catholic Chapel." Others declared it to be a "handsome Doric Column."

Permission was granted to put pumps on the Common "provided the charge of the same be defrayed by private subscription."

1793 JANUARY 24.

A grand citizens parade and civic feast celebrated the French struggle for civil liberty. An ox, also wagons, filled with bread loaves, were in the procession, which beginning at the foot of Middle Street, passed through various streets to the Common, stopping at State Street where the ox was roasted and hogsheads of punch drank.

SEPTEMBER 16.

Four men and five women were placed on the gallows, on the Neck.

OCTOBER 8.

General John Hancock, the First Federal Governor of the Commonwealth—whose bold, dashing signature is seen on the Declaration of Independence, died at the age of fifty-six. An immense concourse of military and citizens attended the funeral in the Granary Burying Ground.

OCTOBER 14.

Funeral of John Hancock. "The procession moved, at two o'clock from the Mansion House of the late Governor Hancock; around the Common, and down Frog Lane (Boylston Street) to Liberty Pole; through the Main Street—and round the State House—up Court Street—and from thence to the place of interment."

The John Hancock inventory contains the clause: "The pasture, adjoining the garden and Beacon Hill, between the mansion and D. D. Rogers, £3000."

During the Hancock administration (1780-1793) Rachell Whall was hung, on the Common, for highway robbery. She had grabbed a bonnet, worth seventy-five cents, from another woman and ran away.

Edward Vaile Brown was hung, on the Common, for committing burglary at the house of Captain Osias Goodwin, on Charles Street, and stealing different household articles.

1794 FEBRUARY 3.

Three pirates—Collins, Poleski and Fertidi—were hung on the Common.

July 30.

A large fire, extending to Russia Wharf at the water's edge, destroyed nearly 100 houses and stores, including six rope walks, which, by kind permission of the authorities, were allowed to be rebuilt at the foot of the Common. The owners paying no rent or taxes.

The town granted to the sufferers by the fire "a piece of marshlands and flats at the bottom of the Common, including such parts of Fox Hill as shall fall within the prescribed boundaries." These flats were then regarded as the boundary of the Common. The grant was made during a period of much excitement and sympathy, the prospective value of the land not being thought of, and was also perpetual. Their reclamation could only be effected by compromise.

The Massachusetts Historical Society collections contain a description of the Common, viz.: "The Common is a spacious, square level spot of ground, below Beacon Hill, and to the east of it. It contains about fifty-five acres, and is a fine grazing pasture for the town's cattle. On days of public festivity, the militia and military corps repair to the Common for the purpose of parading and performing their military manoeuvres. On such occasions it is thronged with all ranks of citizens. The lower classes divert themselves with such pastimes as suit their particular inclination. A number of tents or temporary booths are put up, and furnished with food and liquor for those who require refreshments and can pay for it......

"The Mall is on the eastern side of the Common, in length one thousand, four hundred and ten feet, divided into two walks, parallel to each other; separated by a row of trees. On the outside of each walk is also a row of trees which agreeably shade them. The inhabitants of the town resort thither in the morning and evening of the warm seasons of the year, for the benefit of the fresh air and a pleasant walk. It is fanned by refreshing breezes from a part of Charles River which extends round the bottom of the Common. From the Mall is a pleasing prospect, over the river, of the adjacent city."

A Windmill was set up on the Necklands.

1795 MAY 15.

Ground was broken for the State House on Beacon Hill.

JUNE 1.

A new Amphitheatre was established, at the foot of the Mall, near the Common.

JULY 4.

The cornerstone of the new State House was laid when the ceremonies, forming a part of the day's celebration, drew many to the Common.

SEPTEMBER 14.

The frame of the Columbian Museum was raised by Mr. Bowen, at the head of the Mall, on the Common.

NOVEMBER 9.

The Almshouse, Workhouse, and Granary Grounds were sold at public auction.

The town voted to sell the Almshouse, Workhouse, Bridewell and Granary on condition that they should be removed. The buildings remained, however, used for various stores, refreshment stands, etc., for a number of years.

State House built on Beacon Hill.

Deacon John Sullivan hired a well known bell-crier named Wilson to go around to the different schools, ring up the children, and lead them over the Common to "enjoy the new mown hay."

Up to this year the Common was bounded by a fence on the north, east and south sides. The west was covered by marshy flats, the Western Bay and Charles River.

1796 OCTOBER 19.

The State House was built and the dome completed.

The "six acre lot," the park and pasture, that faced the Common and was washed by the waters of the Western Cove, was reconveyed by Copley, the patentee, to Harrison Gray Otis and John Mason. The orchard was Bannister's Gardens, seen in Burgiss map (1728), and the house, it is said, was bounded by Beacon, Walnut and Spruce Streets with the sea rising and ebbing near Spruce Street. No records exist of the conveyance of the six acre lot from Blackstone, nor is there any to Copley. The earliest is a deed recorded by the Brackett's to Williams and Vial (1676) which was conveyed to Thomas Bannister (1709) and from whose heirs, by foreclosures, mortgages and other legal ways, not recorded, it finally came into the possession of Copley (prior to 1770), Mrs. Ann Pollard, in a deposition, (1711) says, "that Blackstone sold his homestead to

Richard Pepys who built a house on the land where her husband was a tenant and, perchance Pepy's may also have lived on the same property. Two ancient houses stood on the Copley estate; in one Copley painted many of his choicest portraits, where his son, the distinguished Chancellor Lyndhurst, was born. Mrs. Ann Pollard was the first of Winthrop's Colony to leap ashore on the Peninsula and who died (1725) at the advanced age of 105. The ground conveyed by Copley was nearly twenty acres, the proprietors being allowed 100 rods below the highest water mark. Pepy's is said to have returned to England on or before the restoration of the Monarchy. He was a cousin of Samuel, and, some think, the author of "Pepy's Diary," and a Judge in Ireland, (1664) Lord Cottenham (Chancellor in 1836-41) is a descendant who succeeded Lyndhurst. Blackstone belonged to the same family as Sir William, whose commentaries on the English laws are known all over the world and who, a son of Charles, was born in London, (1723) (died 1780) William, the first inhabitant, had grandsons, one of whom, a First-Lieutenant, was killed at the seige of Louisburg, (1746). The parentage and birth place of the father, is something of a mystery, though Suffolk Deeds (1653) show that Sarah Blackstone, of New Castle-upon-Tyne, was authorized to collect money and which deeds contain the name of Stevenson who was the first husband of Blackstone's wife. Blackstone received a grant (1638) from the authorities, of fifteen acres at Muddy Brook — now Brookline — which was then a part of Boston, but whether he continued a freeman, not selling his estate, is not proven. Again he is said to have left Shawmut and, taking his library, appurtenances and cattle, moved to Rehoboth, (Spring 1635) where, in a locality a few rods from the Blackstone River and on a declivity sixty feet high, he made his home in a house called "Study Hill," with 200 acres, where he lived until his death (May 26, 1675) having reached the ripe age of four score. During his residence at Study Hill he met Miantonimo, nephew of Canonicus, King of the Narragansetts, Ocamsequin or Massasoit, King of the Wampanoags, and also their sons Canonchet and King Philip. It is thought his influence with his Indian friends averted hostilities among the tribes, which were very prevalent after his death. He made occasional visits to Boston and preached in Providence and Boston, (1695). While at Shawmut he broke in a bull to bit and bridle which he rode over his estate of 750 acres and which he continued to do at Rehoboth. Governor Endicott had married Miss Sarah Stevenson, widow of John (who died in June, 1673). The lands at Rehoboth, comprising 200 acres, were sold by Blackstone's only child John (1693) and purchased by the Whipples by whom they were held until a recent period. The Indians, making a raid, (1676) burned the house, barns and nearly 200 books, with quartos, folios and some Latin works. This was known as one of the few Indian victories near Study Hill. Manuscripts, volumes and valuable historic papers are thought to have been lost in this fire. Blackstone's grave, near the site of his dwelling, is marked by stones at the head and foot, but that he should have more than one monument has long since been suggested. Notwithstanding these records it is also stated that when Blackstone left the Peninsula he moved to Cumberland, Rhode Island, where he built a house and, it is said, raised the first orchard to grow the first yellow-sweet apple. He is said to have made a lasting impression in his words and deeds and was conscientious, noble and generous. He is everywhere admired for his intellectual pursuits, love of nature, cultivation of the earth and subjection of the lords of the pasture to his bidding and the courage of his convictions. His life was one of seclusion, away from the bustle and the turmoil of a busy world. He had relinquished the tyranny of the throne and sought religious freedom, preferring the wilds of the forest to the arbitrary injustice, amid the civilization, of the old world. His name, like that of Mather, Hutchinson, Stoughton, Sewall and Williams passed into history. It is now recalled by a "Bank," a "Street" and a "Square" in Boston.

When Copley agreed to sell the estate, on his departure for England, many years afterward he desired to annul the contract on the ground of not being aware of the contemplated erection of the State House and other improvements.

1797 April 6.

John Stewart was hung, on the Common, for several robberies committed at the house of Captain Rust, on Prince Street. The plunder was hid in a tomb on Copp's Hill where the burglar was traced and caught one stormy night.

June.

Increase Sumner was sworn in office when a large body of citizens, riding in carriages and mounted on horseback, assembled on the Common, and, proceeding to Roxbury, escorted the Governor into town.

July 4.

The first parade of a new cavalry company drew

quite a crowd to the streets when some went to the Common.

OCTOBER 30.

Stephen Smith was hung, on the Common, for arson.

OCTOBER 30.

More criminals were executed on the Common.

A poem entitled "Beacon Hill," by Sarah Wentworth Morton, was published by Messrs. Manning & Loring, in Boston. The opening lines are:

"Far from this spot, ye light delusions, fly,
While fix'd Attention lifts her boundless eye,
O'er Bunker's field each hallow'd view explores,
Sees the twin-rivers lave the purple shores,
Where the high soil disdain'd the trembling flood,
And stain'd the white wave with Britannia's blood.
Unwearying change the sacred scene displays,
Pillar'd with hills, that fling the morning rays,
And glass'd with streams, that through the twilight glade,
Reflect the reddening skies and broider'd shade;
Here the light scyons' wavy beauties flow,
And seem a plumage on the mountain's brow;
There the proud dome o'erlooks the distant mead,
Where the blue Mystic lifts his sparkling head,
Ceres in smiles her liberal treasure yields,
And waves of gold enrich the floating fields."

1798 JANUARY 11.

The State House was first occupied on Beacon Hill.

JUNE 20.

Rev. Jeremy Belknap, D. D. (Presbyterian Church), Boston, died, and was buried in the Granary Burying Ground. A most distinguished clergyman.

1799 JANUARY.

The body of Governor Increase Sumner was buried in the northerly corner of the Granary Burying Ground where the inscription reads: "He was born at Roxbury, November 27, 1746, and died at the same place, June 7, 1799, in the 53rd year of his age."

DECEMBER 24.

The news of the death of Washington was received with universal expressions of sorrow in the city, bells tolled all day while many, with sad faces, walked on the Common.

DECEMBER 24.

Funeral obsequies for the death of Washington caused great crowds on the streets and Common.

CLOSE OF THE 18TH CENTURY.

During the small-pox epidemic infected clothes were spread out, in different places, on the Common. Many victims died and were buried in the Granary or the Burial Ground on the Common.

1800 JANUARY.

The first number of the *Columbian Phoenix and Boston Review* contains an engraving of "The Boston Troops as Reviewed on the Common, on President Adams birthday, October 30, 1799, by his Honor Lieutenant Governor Gill and Major General Elliott, under the command of Brigadier General Winslow." The State House is a prominent centre.

MARCH 11.

An earthquake, doing some damage in town, was felt on the Common.

SEPTEMBER 26.

Billings died in town, who, it was said, first introduced the violincello, which led to the use of the organ in the churches of Boston. His grave is, unmarked, on the Common.

The land lying west of Beacon Hill was called New Boston.

Constables were ordered to patrol the Common evenings.

1802 MAY 18.

A fire occurred in Boston at noon when, it was said, "the alarm was communicated rapidly by the watchmen stationed on Beacon Hill."

The whipping posts stood in different places: One on Queen Street, another on State Street and still another on the Common. A writer saw, from his school windows, a woman brought in an iron cage, stripped to the waist and then made to suffer thirty or forty lashes while the jeers of the mob only partly drowned her screams.

The law against sabbath breakers was enforced to

prevent bathing at the foot of the Common. The following lines appeared in the *Centinal:*

"In superstitious days, 'tis said,
Hens laid two eggs on *Monday,*
Because a hen would lose her head
That laid an egg on Sunday.

Now our wise rulers and the law
Say none shall wash on Sunday;
So Boston folks must dirty go,
And wash them twice on Monday."

The University, and town, of Cambridge, with the suburbs, affords a fine view of the State House lantern.

The even surface of Boston is varied by three hills: Beacon (west), Copps (north) and Fort (east). Beacon takes its name from the Beacon Light, Copp's, for the first owner of the land; a shoemaker and elder of Dr. Mather's church, and Fort from an ancient fort that stood on the site.

Boston was originally called Tri-mountain.

1803 OCTOBER 2.

Samuel Adams, the American patriot and signer of the Declaration of Independence, died, after living a few days past the age of 81, and was buried, amid a vast throng and the tolling of bells, in the "tomb," in the Granary Burying Ground.

1804. AUGUST 1.

A large funeral procession out of respect to the

memory of Alexander Hamilton, killed in a duel with Aaron Burr, caused great crowds on the streets and the Common.

Feuds existed between the North End boys and the "Charlestown boys." Scouts watched the bridge for stray "pigs" and sometimes on a Thursday or Saturday afternoon the rival forces met armed with clubs and snowballs and lead by an appointed "head" engaged in a fierce encounter resulting, oftentimes, in unpleasant injuries. When the "Copp's-hillers" had "fixed" the "pigs" other fights occurred with the "Prince-Streeters," the "Ann Streeters" (a rough set), the "West Enders," the "Fort-Hillers," and the "South Enders." Camps, commanded by "Generals," were erected on the Common where the opposing juvenile forces more than once, met in battle. The amusement, however, became dangerous and was stopped by Mayor Quincy.

"Follow the Leader," played on the Common, became a favorite game and not so dangerous.

1805 June.

A watch house was occupied near the Beacon monument.

Whipping was practiced on a raised platform, on the Common, where criminals, for minor offences, were sometimes made to stand without being lashed.

A petition to the Selectmen, said, that "the Mill Pond, on the Common, is a nuisance, full of petrid fish, dead dogs and cats."

1806 April 16.

A total eclipse of the sun was seen on the Common.

JULY 4.

A bear, brought from the East Indies, who, standing on his hind legs, performed various antics, and also had a fight with a man, was a part of the day's celebration on the Common.

The six rope walks were burned on the Common. Five were rebuilt.

Foot ball and hockey, both favorite games, were played by boys during the summer. In winter, coasting down the hills was much enjoyed on the Common.

Faneuil Hall was enlarged in a double width and a third story. That it would always be a hall of the people was certain as the city charter provides that neither Faneuil Hall nor the Common could ever be sold or rented.

1808 DECEMBER 10.

Governor James Sullivan died, and was buried in the "family tomb" in the Granary Burying Ground. The inscription reads: "Late Governor and Commander in Chief of the Commonwealth of Massachusetts, who departed this life on the tenth day of December, A. D. 1808, aged 64 years."

Boys batted balls up the steep of Beacon Hill, and, descending, prevented their rolling to the bottom.

The view from the top of Beacon Hill was afterwards likened to that seen from the State House dome, with its "scenes of luxuriant fertility," etc.

1809

The Granary house, on the Common, was used for the Storage of potash.

The Granary house was removed to build the Park Street Church on the Common.

The Granary house was moved from the Common to Commercial Point, Dorchester and altered into a hotel.

The uniting of the two branches of the Congregational order—the old and the new—produced a poem entitled, "A Legend of Brimstone Corner," containing the verses:

"The Devil beamed with horrid joy,
Till to the Common's rim they came,
Then chuckled, 'Wait you here, my boy,
For duties now my presence claim
In yonder church on Brimstone Corner,
Where Pleasure's dead and lacks a mourner.'

And that is why the faithful Gale
Round Park Street Corner still must blow,
Waiting for him with horns and tail,
At least some people tell me so,
None of your famous antiquarians,
But just some wicked Unitarians."

The Park Street Church was built.

1810 July 4.

It was voted by the town to open a new burial ground on the Neck.

Two pirates—Sam Tully and a companion named Dalton—were sentenced to be hung at Roxbury Neck on the Peninsula, South Boston. Dalton got a reprieve on the gallows and became a Methodist or Baptist preacher.

An old tavern, called the Roebuck, stood on a narrow, curved, lane leading out of Ann Street, where a murder was committed by two Danish or Swedish sailors—John P. Rog and Nils Peterson—both—with two others, were hanged on Roxbury Neck when pedlars sold "pairs of verses." Two lines were:

"And, oh, the cruel murderers! it was a dreadful din,
The one he took a loggerhead, another, a rolling pin."

The tide rose over Charles Street making a swamp with salt-water grass at the lower end of the Common.

People leaving the Common would often cross to the Washington Garden—on Colonnade Row, nearly opposite the Park Street Church—a favorite resort for open air concerts, ice cream, lemonade with sticks and flirtations.

Once or twice a year a parade celebrated the "Feast of Squantum" when the best people of the town performed Indian rites. Mounted cavaliers, wearing white top boots and spurs, rode back and forth over the Common.

The Mall around the Common was nearly completed by private subscription.

1811 April 30.

Rev. Joseph Eckley, pastor of the Old South Church died, and was buried in the Granary Burying Ground.

Beacon Hill was a favorite resort for the people of Boston as well as strangers.

The brick monument was taken down on Beacon Hill and the hill levelled.

The highest part of Beacon Hill was dug down for dwellings.

1812 August 31.

The Salem Light Infantry came to return the visit of the Boston Light Infantry and pitched their tents on the Common and were reviewed, by the Governor, on Fort Hill in the afternoon.

November 25.

A petition, signed by many inhabitants, remonstrated against further executions on the Common and which was granted by the board.

The sails of the frigate Constitution (Old Ironsides) that figured in the war with England when "Her thunders shook the mighty deep," were made, by consent of Mr. Bulfinch, at the Granary, on the Common, where the spacious floor gave ample room to spread.

The military companies were the New England Guards and the Rifle Rangers. Also the Sea Fencibles, Captain Winston Lewis, a ship chandler on State Street, which composed of sailors, was organized early in the war. Their headquarters was at the Gunhouse at the foot of the Common. There was not much soldiering in these days, though Nigger 'Lection and Fourth of July drew out a good number of uniformed companies, and the Ancient and Honorable paraded on Artillery Election Day. The Governor, before the organization of the Lancers, also was always escorted by a company of Cavalry to Cambridge on Commencement Day.

During the war a quantity of cannons were kept on the corner of the Common (Tremont Street).

1813 MAY 21.

Apprehensions for an attack on the Maine border led to a guard being ordered for the Park Artillery "to parade at the Gunhouse on the Common, at seven o'clock, on Saturday evening next, with their side arms and in their uniforms complete."

JUNE.

The *Polyanthus* contains an aqua-tint of a "View on Boston Common," which (1910) was exhibited in the Boston Athenaeum.

Dr. Joy died, at South Boston Point, in the house he had once built, on the Copley estate, when he wished a country home, saying it "being country enough for him," and it was said "he was right in believing that nowhere else could he inhale purer breezes than those which were wafted across the Boston Common and the river that then washed its borders." The noxious exhalations of the Back Bay do not, even now, reach the Common.

1814

APRIL 10.

A report that a British fleet was off the cost of Boston led the authorities to make great preparations for defence causing much excitement in town and on the Common.

APRIL 13.

A reward of one hundred dollars was offered, by the Selectmen, for the arrest of grave robbers at the South Burying Grounds.

APRIL 23.

The *Boston Gazette* announces a procession of the Washington Benevolent Society, on the 30th, "the route of the procession will be from the State House to the Common, thence, across the Common to Boylston Street.

MAY 10.

Oliver H. Perry; the hero of Lake Erie, visited Boston and the Common.

MAY 10.

Commodore Perry was a guest of honor and tendered a grand dinner in Boston upon which occasion he was escorted by the Rangers, Winslow Blues, New England Guards and Boston Light Infantry all drawn up on the Common. Guests, who assembled at the State House, crossed to the upper part of the enclosure.

MAY 11.

Robert Treat Paine, signer of the Declaration of Independence, died and was buried in the Granary Burying Ground.

JUNE 15.

A religious Festival was held to celebrate Europe's triumph over the despotism of military power. It proved a melancholy affair. The *Independent Chronicle,* says: "Ten thousand persons to assemble in the open Common, to look at 2600 lamps burning in the windows of the State House was a ludicrous display of festivity." The day was closed by fireworks on the Common while the Hancock and Bowdoin mansions were highly illuminated.

SEPTEMBER 6.

More apprehensions of an attack on the Maine border led to detachments of Military being encamped on the Common.

Captain Osgood, who commanded the Militia, on the Common, applied for "100 kettles, 200 pans, 100 pint pots, 32 axes, 32 spades, straw and wood."

The Boston and Albany Mill Corporation projected building a dam with passenger way overhead which called forth a loud protest from a citizen in the *Advertiser,* viz.: "Have you ever visited the Mall; have you ever inhaled the Western breeze, fragrant with perfume, refreshing every sense, and invigorating every nerve? What think you of converting the beautiful sheet of water which skirts the Common into an empty mud basin, reeking with filth, abhorrent to the smell, and distasteful to the eye? By every god of sea, lake, or fountain, it is incredible."

1815 MONDAY, FEBRUARY 13.

Josiah P. Quincy, says, "When the news of peace

came it was just after breakfast we set forth in the sleigh and went through Cornhill, then past the Common and through the Main Street down to the North End. The streets were crowded with people, flags waved from every house and across the streets.

FEBRUARY 13.

General Jackson's victory at New Orleans was celebrated by the firing of salutes from the Forts and the artillery on the Common.

SEPTEMBER.

A terrific gale destroyed a great many trees with several of the Paddock elms on the Common.

OCTOBER 22.

Many townspeople went to the Common and into the country to get fresh air on account of a stringent Sunday law.

Beacon Street was widened, 17 feet, by cutting off a strip of land at the State House, and, 20 feet, at a point at Belknap Street.

Hancock Avenue was sometimes called Cato Alley affording, by mutual consent with the authorities, a convenient access, to and fro, across the Common.

1816 JANUARY 4.

Rev. John Lathrop, D. D., Second Church, Boston, died, and was buried in the Granary Burying Ground.

Several paths were laid out and improved on the Common.

Beacon Street Mall was laid out.

1817 MARCH 13.

Henry Phillips was hung, on Boston Neck, for the murder of Gaspard Denegri, near Roebuck Tavern, in January. "After the cap was drawn over his eyes he sang a song of three verses, dropped the handkerchief, and was launched into eternity."

MARCH 13.

The gallows were moved to the South End, near Garland Street, on the Neck.

JULY.

President Monroe visited Boston when the address of welcome was delivered by Harrison Gray Otis after which he was escorted by a grand procession through the city. The *Boston Commercial* (of the 3d) says, the procession passed "through Boylston Street, to an opening in the Common, between the Mall and Gunhouse, through lines formed by the scholars of the different schools in Boston, attended by their several instructors, northwardly, over the Common, towards the State House, to a point opposite the west end of Winter Street," the number of spectators on the streets, and on the Common exceeded any reception since that of the "Sainted Washington."

AUGUST 22.

John Quincy Adams, says in his *Memoirs* that after an absence of eight years from Boston, having been in Europe and in Washington, he walked "round the city," with his friend Mr. Foster, observing with pleasure the masses of new buildings on the Central Wharf, New

Cornhill and Common Street, and that the only alteration causing him regret was the demolition of Beacon Hill.

SEPTEMBER 7.

An earthquake, which threw down several chimneys, was felt on the Common.

DECEMBER 5.

The Book of Days, by Harriet Porter Beecher, describes Litchfield, Connecticut, saying, its beauty consists in the wide streets shaded, on either side, by fine trees excelling in pleasantness any she had ever seen except on Boston Mall.

A "Description of Boston," by Shaw, contains a View of Boston Common.

1818 MAY 10.

Paul Revere, died at his home on Charter Street, Boston, and was buried, in the "Revere Family Tomb" in the Granary Burying Ground. The grave is situated in the rear of the centre and where a low raised stone bears the simple inscription: "Paul Revere, born in Boston, January, 1735, died May, 1818." He was intimately acquainted with James Otis, John Adams, Samuel Adams, Joseph Warren and other Revolutionary patriots and shared their fame.

MAY 20.

A small fish sensation, near the Frog Pond, on the Common.

1819 FEBRUARY 18.

Four pirates, John Williams, John P. Rog, Niles Peterson and Francis Frederick, were hung on Boston Neck.

William Johnson was sent to State Prison for life. He decoyed a countryman to the Common under pretence of selling his squirrels and then robbed him of them.

The five rope walks were burned on the Common.

James Gordon Bennett, a rising young journalist was often seen walking on the Common.

1820 MAY 25.

Michael Powers was hung for murder on the Neck.

JUNE 25.

Holmes and two other pirates were hung on the Neck.

Dr. Hale, who "playing soldier" in what was left of the old redoubts on Flagg-Staff Hill also describes the Common at about this time, viz.: (1) A pasture for cows, (2) a playground for children, (3) a place for beating carpets, (4) a training ground for the militia.

The "City Criers House" where criers, with bells in hand, went forth through the streets of the town and across the Common.

Among the prominent residents who, at this time or subsequently, lived on Summer Street, or in the neighborhood, some of whom had died, were: John Adams, Charles Francis Adams, Brooks Adams, Samson Reed,

Samuel Salisbury, Frederick William Geyer, Samuel P. Gardner, Ebenezer Preble, Nathaniel I. Bowditch, Rev. William Emerson, Dr. Nathaniel Frothingham, Robert C. Winthrop, Drs. Harwood and Jacob Bigelow, Rev. Drs. Frothingham and Kirkland, Chief Justice Isaac Parker, the distinguished surgeon Henry J. Bigelow, Rev. Rufus Ellis, Rev. William B. O. Peabody and George Cabot. All were often seen on the Common.

Washington, Little and Flagstaff Hills on the Common.

1821 AUGUST 8.

The West Point Cadets were encamped on the Common.

The opening of the Mill Dam, on Western Avenue, drew an immense concourse to the Common.

1822 MARCH 7.

Gilbert Close and Samuel Clisby were hung on the Necklands near the burying ground. Their offense was highway robbery, they robbed Ezra Haynes, a citizen, on Cambridge Street, on the tenth of August.

MARCH 7.

Great excitement was caused by graves robbed on the Neck.

APRIL 25.

Samuel Green was hung, on the Necklands, for killing "Billy" Williams in November. The murder was committed in the State Prison.

April 25.

Gallows were erected, on the Neck, until the close of the year.

June 15.

As the firing of cannon, on the Common, disturbed the surrounding neighborhood, the *Columbian Centinel,* says, a request was sent to the Commanders to "avoid all unnecessary use of the Malls in the performance of their military duties; and that all firing on training day should be done as remotely from public highways as can be......and that this part of military duty should be done south-westerly to the great tree."

An ordinance prohibiting the shaking of carpets on the Common drew forth a newspaper article, by Edward Everett Hale, entitled "The Last Shake."

When Boston became a city the charter protected the Common from either sale or lease.

1823 March 24.

The lands of the Public Garden were offered for sale.

May 13.

It was required that all cows, roaming at large, must wear a "Tally" on the neck, and that no person should pasture more than one cow on the Common.

May 23.

John Phillips, First Mayor of Boston, died, and was buried in the Granary Burying Ground. He was father of the great anti-slavery orator, Wendell Phillips.

The sympathetic feelings of Charles Sumner are shown by an incident when a ragged beggar boy, with basket on his arm, passed a group of boys playing on the Common, when one asked him—"Who patched your pants?" "My mother!" replied the boy. "Well you had better go home and tell her to mend your jacket!" A few moments after the beggar boy had passed along, Sumner had left the group and was seen walking away. Another boy, who had slipped out of the party, met him, crying, and asked—"What's the matter, Charlie?" when Sumner replied,—"How unkind it was to ridicule a poor beggar boy because he wore ragged clothes, perhaps his parents can not afford to buy him better ones!"

Paddock's Mall was ordered to be paved with cobble stones.

1824 JUNE 29.

Charles Street Mall was laid out.

JULY 7.

Just before two o'clock the alarm bells drew the engines to a fire in Mr. Bryant's new house, carpenter shops and other premises on Charles and Chestnut Streets. The wind blew a hurricane as the fire was watched by many persons on the Beacon Street Mall where women and children at a moment's warning were compelled to flee for safety. Many household appurtenances, from kitchen utensils to elaborate carpets and handsome ornaments were hurried to the Common to escape the flames and from some houses which they did not reach. Seven dwellings were burned on Beacon Street, and it was only owing to the open space of the Common that the southern portion of the city was saved.

Tuesday, August 22.

General Lafayette visited Boston when the streets, through which the procession walked, were gayly decorated with French and American flags. The General was presented by Governor Eustis to Mayor Quincy and a charming incident of the reception was "the singing of the *Marseillaise* by a throng of school children on the Common."

The *Columbian Centinel,* (of the 25th), says: "—passed through the Common on which were placed, extending the whole length of it, in two lines, the pupils of the Public Schools, the misses principally dressed in white, and the lads in blue coats and white underclothes, each bearing a portrait of Lafayette on their breasts, stamped on ribbons. They exceeded 2500 in number. —On passing the line a beautiful little girl, about six years old, stepped forth, and begged leave to address the General. She was handed to the Mayor, and by him to the General, who saluted her. She then delivered a short address, took a wreath of flowers from her head, and put it on his head. The General made her a very affectionate reply, and placed the wreath in his carriage.

There were over seventy thousand spectators.

Cards of admission were required for the various reviews, on the Common, when people entered Beacon Street and the Frog Pond.

Lafayette, while in Boston, stayed at a boarding house that stood on the site of the first Almshouse.

The *Boston Monthly Magazine* contains an article by "A Boston Visitor," who says: "repaired to the Common, so famous for its command of picturesque scenery —there I saw another and larger, collection of people.

The green, from the State House to the Mall, was full of troops and spectators. The Mall was covered with Masons, deeply arranged in close order, and every street and habitation in the vicinity was crowded with a dense population. About ten, the Grand Lodge and Royal Arch Chapter entered the Mall and joined the rest of the fraternity......Scarcely were these fraternities organized into a procession, under the shady trees of the Mall, before several handsome companies of light infantry, on the Common, opened to the right and left, —the troop of horse rode rapidly past them and a number of carriages approached the avenue. The bugle, horns and drums resounded, and the whole band of music performed a salute as Lafayette, drawn in a barouche, with four white horses, and a number of cars carrying distinguished individuals and old soldiers of Bunker Hill passed along......The survivors of Bunker Hill were about forty......At last, an excellent band of music struck up a National air which dissipated my serious meditations. The procession moved, and successive bodies, in deep array, marched from the Mall to the consecrated spot."

Many years afterward Wendell Phillips, who, a boy of fourteen, stood, with the school children, on the Common, alluded to the occasion in a charming address to other school children who were gathered in Music Hall, viz.:—"I was a little boy in a class in the Latin School at the time and we were turned out on yonder Common in a grand procession, at nine o'clock in the morning. And for what? Not to hear music—no; but for something better than music, that thrilled more than eloquence—a sight which should live in the memory forever, the best sight which Boston ever saw—the welcome of Lafayette on his return to this country, after an absence of a score of years. I can boast boys and girls, more than you. I can boast that these eyes have beheld the hero of three revolutions, this hand has touched the right hand that held up Hancock and Washington. Not all this glorious celebration can equal that glad reception of the Nation's benefactor by all that Boston could offer him—a sight of her children. It was a long procession, and, unlike other processions we started punctually at the hour published. They would not let us wander about and did not wish us to sit down—I then received my first lesson in hero-worship. I was so tired after four hours' waiting I could scarcely stand; but when I saw him—that glorious old Frenchman; I could have stood until today.

Lafayette, when he visited Boston, said "The world should never forget the spot where once stood 'Liberty Tree,' so famous in your annals."

The Julien House, in Milk Street, stood, an antiquated building for over thirty years. It was a noted restaurant and derived its name from its proprietor, Mon. Jean-Baptiste Gilbert Payplat dis Julien. Many a Bostonian having partaken of a breakfast or luncheon afterwards walked down to the Common.

Band concerts were given, on the Common, during the summer months.

The city purchased the flatlands, at the bottom of the Common, for $50,000.

President Quincy planted two rows of elms greatly adding to the beauty of the Park Street Mall.

The Charles Street Mall was completed during the first year of the administration of Mayor Quincy—the elder.

1825 MAY.

The Ghingo was planted "on each side of the Neck."

JUNE 17.

The semi-centennial celebration of the battle of Bunker Hill was one of the grandest events that ever occurred in Boston. General Lafayette sat on the platform, with other dignitaries, listened to the eloquent oration of Daniel Webster. The crowd was great. One authority says that "everything that has wheels, and everything that has legs, used them to get to Boston. The head of the civil and military procession reached the site of the monument—Charlestown Square—before the rear had started from the Common. At four o'clock the distinguished guests mounted on a platform in the middle of the Frog Pond, and an immense concourse covered the slopes, of the Common, listening to addresses from Mayor Josiah Quincy, Jr., and other speakers. The close of the day was feelingly alluded to in the words: "The sun was just sinking below the horizon, and its last rays tinged the summit of the watery column, the bells began to ring, cannon were fired, and rockets streamed across the sky. To the multitude, around, the scene was one of intense interest and excitement, which it is impossible to describe, but which no one can forget. After the first moment of surprise most of the spectators looked around upon the neighbors, some laughed aloud, the men swung their hats and shouted, and some men wept."

The remains of Major General Joseph Warren, identified, (by a nephew—Dr. John C. Warren—and Paul Revere) "by the eye tooth and the fatal bullet behind the left ear" were placed in a hard wood box and removed from the Minot Tomb, in the Granary Burying Ground, to the Warren Tomb in St. Paul's Church, Boston.

1826 MARCH 3.

John Holland was hung, on the Neck, for the murder of a man named Houghton, a watchman.

MAY.

Park Street Mall laid out.

MAY.

Frog Pond curbed and improved.

AUGUST.

Funeral obsequies for the death of Presidents Adams and Jefferson drew great crowds to the streets and Common.

OCTOBER 13.

John Tileston (Master Johnny) a well-known school master, especially to all the boys and girls, whose school was located on the west corner of Prince and Margaret Streets (which old wooden building, turned into a grocery is still standing) died, in his 92nd year and was buried in the Granary Burying Ground. His portrait hangs in the collection at the Boston Museum.

OCTOBER 30.

Macready the great tragedian says, in his Reminiscences—"led me to Boston, when upon the same terms, £50 per night, I represented the same plays, using my leisure days in making acquaintances with Bunker's or rather Breed's Hill, Faneuil Hall, the Capitol, the Common and the various institutions and sites that laid claim to my attention.

The poplar trees, which had long disfigured the Park Street Mall, were cut down and replaced by elms.

1827 MARCH 1.

Governor Christopher George died, aged 68, and was buried in the Granary Burying Ground. "His mind was acute and discriminating; his morals pure; his manners dignified and elegant."

APRIL 28.

A new regulation was made compelling constables to patrol the Common in the day time.

MAY 18.

Liquor was forbidden to be sold, on the Common, on public days.

JUNE 15.

An obelisk, of Quincy granite, was erected in memory of the parents of Benjamin Franklin, in the Granary Burying Ground. A bronze plate on the front side bears the name Franklin and a tablet sunk underneath, revives the inscription on the original stone erected by Benjamin Franklin, viz.: "Josiah Franklin and Abiah his wife, lie here interred. They lived lovingly together in wedlock fifty-five years, and without estate, or any gainful employment, by constant labor and honest industry, maintained a large family comfortably, and brought up thirteen children and seven grandchildren reputably. From this instance, Reader, Be encouraged to diligence in thy calling, and distrust not Providence. He was a pious and prudent man. She a discreet and virtuous woman. Their youngest son, in filial regard to their memory, places this stone. J. F., born 1655, died 1744, a. e. 89. A. F., born 1667, died 1752, a. e. 85."

And also: "The original inscription having been nearly obliterated a number of citizens erected this monument as a mark of respect for the illustrious author MDCCCXXVII." The corner stone contains an inscribed silver plate, a "Franklin" with several other medals, the silver plate reads: "This monument was erected over the remains of the parents of Benjamin Franklin, by the citizens of Boston, from respect to the private character and public services of the illustrious patriot and philosopher, and for the many tokens of his affectionate attachment to his native town."

The obelisk was unveiled with appropriate ceremonies.

August 11.

Palm leaf hats were first worn and frequently seen on the Common.

October 31.

A marble statue of Washington was placed in the State House.

DECEMBER 17.

Thirteen acres of land were reserved for a nursery on the Necklands.

Cows were pastured on the Neck, at eight dollars for the season.

1829 APRIL 22.

A new ordinance read that Common Street, from Court, by the Common, to Washington, should be called Tremont Street.

JULY 4.

Gambling and liquor stands were driven away, by Constables, from the Common.

JULY 4.

The day was quietly celebrated—"On the Common no liquor, no booths and no people. At the Washington Gardens, afternoon, Orator Emmons held forth in flights of passing eloquence and rhyme, which, with a nondescript fish, were all to be heard and seen for four pence."

DECEMBER.

Excitement caused by grave robberies on the Neck.

On Election day rows of stands ran beside the wooden fence from Park to West Street, and even farther, on the Common, where beverages and eatables were bought from white and colored stand keepers. Oysters in saucers that cost fo' pence ha' penny (six and a quarter cents) were sold, besides lobsters, candy, cakes, doughnuts, gingernuts, lemonade, spruce beer, ginger beer, etc. Colored women, wearing gay colored handkerchiefs tied around their heads, resembling typical Southern negresses, pushed hand carts containing an ample supply of cakes, buns, jumbles, waffles, seed cakes, President biscuit, baked beans, hot brown bread, etc., about the Common.

William Lloyd Garrison while confined in a Baltimore jail during that period of festivity called "Election Week!" showed his admiration for Boston in writing some verses about the Common.

1830 MAY 10.

The city authorities passed a resolution forbidding cows on the Common.

MAY.

The Society for the Suppression of Intemperance offered a petition to the city for a band of music, on the Common, during the afternoon and evening of the Fourth of July—"Such a practice having, in their judgment, a tendency to promote order and suppress an inclination to riot and intemperance." The petition was granted.

MAY.

The Ghingo was planted in the Granary Burying Ground.

MAY.

Many trees were planted in the Granary Burying Ground.

JULY 7.

The Common: "Under Mayor Quincy there were "no tables groaning under the weight of ponderous hams and tender pigs,—no barrows,—no dice tables,—no wheels of fortune,—no casting at the black joke."

SEPTEMBER 17.

Josiah Quincy, in an address to the citizens of Boston, at the close of the second centennial settlement of the city referred to "The lofty heights, that the march of progress has obliterated, where from the lone cottage of Blackstone smoke was seen ascending out of the chimney and where the Beacon fire rallied the neighboring population when any danger threatened the metropolis.

SEPTEMBER 17.

The 200th Anniversary of the settlement of Boston; pupils and instructors from all the schools met on the Common, at nine o'clock to take part in exercises.

No cows were permitted to graze on the Common.

Edward Everett Hale, in a beautiful story of this period, tells of several boys watching a fire, just above the Frog Pond, on a winter's day. One boy, handed a hatchet, is told to go and fetch two, or three, more cedars! The boys are joined by other comrades, one with a leather satchel, hung on his back, with three flounders. Two more came with red skins full of clams, all being cooked when the stones were hot enough. Another brought two lobsters which were put in the pot hanging over the fire. An Indian boy, Charles King,—with basket slung on his back, now joined the party. He had found the place before while fishing and had brought them to a secluded spot. The fire started, the boys, who had begged a half holiday, ran off to play returning to eat dinner which was eaten under a great boulder, slate stones and clams were used for plates, two or three Sheffield whittles for knives and fingers supplying the place of forks. Water was drawn through the ice on the Frog Pond. A game of ball unearthed a red fox from his hole when all the boys started in pursuit and, covering a large space found another shelter where he was seized and poked with sticks by the leaders, while the smaller boys, out of breath, had returned to the fire on the Common.

The Parks, or Malls, on Charles, Beacon, Park and Tremont Streets, contain 550 trees.

There is a small marble monument and some gravestones on the Common Burial Ground. Many of the graves are those of Roman Catholics.

It was proposed to change the name of the Common and Malls to Washington Park. This was met by a loud public protest.

1831 AUGUST 23.

Funeral obsequies for the death of President Monroe drew great crowds to the streets and Common.

SEPTEMBER.

Some constables patrolled the Common by day.

NOVEMBER.

The inside fence, on the east side, was removed from the Common.

1832. APRIL.

Dead cats and old boots made an unsightly appearance on the Common.

1833 JUNE 1.

A fight between constables and gamblers occurred on the Common.

JUNE.

President Jackson was honored by a large reception. The *Columbian Centinel* (21st) says: "The procession will move through Washington Street and Boylston Street to the Common, when the instructors and pupils of the Public Schools will be placed in line, in front of the Fire Department. On arriving at the bottom of the Common the cavalcade and carriages will proceed up Tremont Street as far as St. Paul's, while the remainder of the procession crosses the Common to the head of Winter Street."

OCTOBER 22.

Henry Clay visited Boston and the Common.

NOVEMBER 13.

The great meteoric shower was seen in Boston and by any person who chanced to be on the Common late at night. It looked as if "all the stars were falling down."

A little Boston boy, awaking at night, thought that the stars were all falling and told his father who, thinking he had been dreaming, bade him, "go to sleep!" The boy had seen the meteoric shower.

The Old Tree on the Common measures 24 feet in circumference at the base and 17.6 feet above the ground.

America and the Americans—inscribed to Lafayette by "A Citizen of the world" London, says: "Boston, which has been founded two centuries was originally called Tremont, or Tre-mountain, from the circumstance of its being situated on three hills. The city is almost surrounded by water; the connection with the main land being formed by a narrow strip called the Neck. The communication, in other directions, is kept up by timber bridges; one of which is no less than 1300 yards in length. The older streets are irregular...... In front of the State House is a park, many acres in extent, which, in colonial times, bore the name of the Common; but having been railed and ornamented, is now dignified by the title of Mall. Here the British troops were for some time encamped, and near a huge and ancient elm, which still spreads its venerable arms, are the remains of a redoubt, thrown up at that period. Among the number of mansions, which form one side of the streets bounding through beautiful verdant enclosure, that of the celebrated patriot, Hancock, is distinguished."

1834 MAY.

Many trees were planted, by Superintendent Hughes, on the Neck.

JULY 4.

A feast celebrated the christening of the Whig party when two thousand persons sat under a tent on the Common.

JULY 4.

A large Whig Festival was held on the Common when a Pavilion to hold 2500 persons was erected on the Mall. The *Columbian Centinel* (9th) says: "The interior of the Pavilion was decorated by National flags, patriotic banners, pendents, festoons and a profusion of flowers, and the revered name of Washington and Lafayette, of Hancock and Adams, and other heroes and statesmen, of Revolutionary memory, appeared conspicuous. The centre of the Pavilion was supported by a grand Liberty Pole eighty feet in heighth."

JULY 31.

Durant—an areonaut—made an ascension from the Common.

SEPTEMBER 6.

Funeral solemnities for the death of Lafayette drew great crowds to the streets and Common.

Emerson, in one of his "Journals," says: "I rejoice in Time. I do not cross the Common without a wild poetic delight, notwithstanding the prose of my demeanor. Thank God I live in this country."

And again: "Knowledge transfers the censorship from the State House to the reason of every citizen and compels every man to mount guard over himself, and puts to shame and remorse for sergeants and maces."

1835 MAY 8.

The hill of Gardner Greene, Esq., was demolished when the Ghingo Tree (China) was removed from Pemberton Hill to the Beacon Street Mall.

JULY 4.

Lauriatt—aeronaut—made an ascension from the Common.

JULY 4.

Fireworks on the Common were spoiled by the rain.

OCTOBER 21.

William Lloyd Garrison edited an abolition paper called the *Liberator*. This outspoken sheet had caused much criticism when it was declared that Southern merchants would not trade in Boston if a paper, like the *Liberator,* was permitted to attack and malign their institutions. A mob threatened to seize the editor and suppress the paper! A large crowd assembled on the northwest corner of Court and Washington Streets, where they were addressed by Mayor Lyman (whom it was thought should have ordered out the military) from the steps of the building. He advised them all, quietly, to depart to their homes, though about seventy-five men marched, in single file, upstairs to the editor's office on the third floor, they soon returned crying out that Garrison was not there, but had retreated out the rear doors into State Street where he was found, and now, pursued by the mob, escaped into the Old State House amid threats to "seize him!' "lynch him!" Garrison was finally got into a coach and driven to the jail on Leverett Street. The mob dispersed in less than an hour some walking about the streets, others loitering on the Common.

The buildings, standing on the Common, were disappearing one after another.

The City Tavern was a rendezvous for the theatrical companies, and many an actor was seen lounging, dozing or smoking in the bar-room, or walking on the Common, during the day.

The American House was opened and on the list of guests are found the names of Ralph Waldo Emerson and Walt Whitman both of whom once walked, arm in arm, on the Common, discussing the feasibility of publishing *Leaves of Grass.*

The Common was the great feature and pride of Boston where strangers paused to look with expressions of admiration and delight.

1836 JULY 4.

A feature of the day's celebration was the liberty of the Common to colored people, who, up to this time, were only allowed its advantages on "Nigger 'Lection day."

A large number of school girls dressed in white, carried moss, baskets in various designs, which were afterwards sold, the sales one day amounting to $1,000.

JULY 13.

People walking on the Common were reminded of a change when the church bells rang at *one o'clock,* instead of *twelve.*

JULY.

Funeral honors for the death of President Madison caused many to gather on the streets and Common.

AUGUST.

Boylston Street Mall was laid out.

AUGUST.

Some boys were fined for bathing in the Frog Pond on the Common.

Colonel Henry Lee who was graduated at Harvard in the class of this year, referred long afterwards to "the fortification on the Common that was levelled while I was in College."

The Boylston Street Mall was extended through the burial ground where two rows of tombs were closed.

Impressions of America—(1833-'34, 35) by Tyrone Power, Esq., vol. 1, London, says:—"The approach to Boston, either by sea or land, gives to it an extremely bold and picturesque character. It is spread over a series of lofty heights, nearly insulated, and is surrounded by a marshy level running from the highlands on the main, to which the city is united by a very narrow isthmus to the southward. The lofty dome of its State House, and the numerous spires and towers of its churches, rising between two and three hundred feet above the surrounding level of either land or sea, combine to produce a *coup d'oeil* more imposing than is presented by either New York or Philadelphia.

The streets of the city generally are narrow and irregular, following the windings of the lofty hills on which it is spread, and having more the air of an old English country town than any place I have yet seen in the country. . . . . . The most modern quarter of the city lies to the west, surrounding the park, or common, as it is termed,—an ancient reserve of some sixty acres, the property of the citizens, beautifully situated and tastefully laid out. It is bordered on the lower side by a mall of venerable looking elms; has a pretty pond of water under a rising ground near its centre, the remains of an English fort; and open to the front is the Charles River. On three sides, this common is flanked by very fine streets, having houses of the largest class, well built, and kept with a right English spirit as far as regards the scrupulous cleanliness of the entrances, areas, and windows. The English are a window cleaning race, and nowhere have I observed this habit so closely inherited as here. Overlooking this common, too, is the State House, and on a line with it, the mansion of its patriot founder, Mr. Hancock, a venerable stone built edifice, raised upon a terrace withdrawn a few yards from the line of the present street. The generous character of its first owner has made this house an object of great interest, and it is to be hoped the citizens will look carefully to its preservation as a worthy fellow to *Faneuil Hall, for by no one was the 'cradle of Liberty' more carefully tended than by the owner of 'Hancock House.' "

JUNE 14.

The first parade of the National Lancers caused great crowds on the streets and Common.

*Foot Note: "Faneuil Hall, so-called, the old Town Hall—a spot dedicated by the Bostonians to the recollections of their country's first struggle for independence, and greatly venerated."

JUNE 30.

A new flag staff was erected, near the Old Elm, on the Common.

JUNE.

A riot called the "Broad Street Riot" occurred which was caused by the firemen attempting to pass through the carriages of an Irish funeral proceeding to the grave. A general fight ensued when sticks and stones were used and many were seriously bruised, but no lives were lost. The military suppressed the riot which had already grown large and formidable. The whole Fire Department was disbanded as a result of the *melee*. Groups loitered on the Common.

JULY 5.

It was decided to move the edge stones about the Frog Pond.

SEPTEMBER 12.

A general military review took place, on the Common, when the Montgomery Guards came, causing fire companies to leave the line. The review was postponed.

OCTOBER 20.

Lands were granted by the authorities to Horace Gray for the Public Garden.

OCTOBER 30.

The city was visited by a deputation composed of delegates of four different tribes—the Sacs and Foxes with Black Hawk, and the Sioux and Iowa, who came to Boston and erected a camp on the Common. During their stay they gave a war dance when they appeared dressed in the skins of wild animals with horns, and, wielding pointed weapons, created much alarm by their grotesque manoeuvres and frantic shrieks, among the 70,000 spectators. When they broke camp they left the city in open barouches, the most hideous sitting in a conspicuous position and wielding a war weapon.

NOVEMBER 2.

Emerson, in one of his "Journals," says, "Immense curiosity in Boston to see the Delegation of the Sacs and Foxes, of the Sioux and the Ioways. I saw the Sacs and Foxes at the State House on Monday, about thirty in number. Edward Everett addressed them, and they replied. One chief said 'They had no land to put their words upon, but they were nevertheless true.' One chief wore the skin of a buffalo's head with the horns attached on his head, others birds with outspread wings. Immense breadth of shoulder and very muscular persons. Our Picts were so savage in their head-dress and nakedness that it seemed as if the bears and catamounts had sent a deputation. They danced a war-dance on the Common, in the centre of the greatest crowd ever seen on that area. The governor cautioned us of the gravity of the tribe, and that we should beware of any expression of the ridiculous, and the people all seemed to treat their guests gingerly, as the keepers of lions and juguars do those creatures whose taming is not quite yet trustworthy. Certainly it is right and natural that the Indian should come and see the civil white men, but this was hardly genuine, but a show; so we were not parties, but spectators. Therefore a man looks up and laughs and meets the eyes of some by-stander who also laughs. Keokuk, Black Hawk, Roaring Thunder. At Faneuil Hall they built a partition between the two tribes because the tribes are at war."

The tribes at war were the Sioux, Sacs and Foxes.

And again:

"George Bradford compares the happiness of Gore Ripley riding the horse to plough, with boys of Boston of his age, who are too old to play on the Common, and who can only dress and fix straps to their pantaloons."

Christopher Gore Ripley was a son of Rev. Samuel Ripley, and, afterwards, Chief Justice of Minnesota.

1838 JULY 4.

Hawthorne, in "American Note Book," says, "Booths on the Common, selling ginger bread, sugar plums, and confectionery, spruce beer, lemonade———on the top of one of the booths, a monkey with a tail two or three feet long..... There are boys going about with molasses candy, almost melted down in the sun. Shows: a mammoth rat, a collection of pirates, murderous and the like, in wax......One or two old salts, rather the worse for liquor, in general the people are temperate."

JULY 4.

Emerson says, in his "Journals"—"The Fourth of July, red with artillery; the Common full of children, the woods full of gunners, and at night the sky crackling with rockets, even down to the Election, miscalled by wanton boys 'Nigger 'Lection.' I have kindly vision out in these lone fields of marching ranks with red facings and white shoes, of boys in vacation; and on such a day as that, I still feel a gayer air."

JULY 24.

A great reception and dinner was given to Daniel

Webster at Faneuil Hall, some afterwards walking down to the Common.

Harriet Martineau, in "Retrospect of Western Travel," says "The ceremonial of Commencement Week (Harvard) was now over; but not the bustle and gaiety. The remaining two days were spent in drives to Boston and to Bunker Hill, and in dinner and evening visits to Judge Story's to some of the professors, and to Mr. Everett's, since governor of the State." The Common was visited.

The shops in Boston are very pretty though they do not equal those on Chestnut Street in Philadelphia. Shoppers often crossed the Common.

Luncheon parties with ham, cheese, beer, crackers and apples would often sit under the trees on the Common.

"Reminiscences of a Walker Around Boston," says, "The three hilled city, with its picturesque inequalities of ground, its glittering spires, its tufts of trees (alas! too rare!) and the State House, diverted by distance, of its architectural errors, crowning the whole, and all reflected upon the clear waters of the bay beneath our feet, now brimming with an overflowing tide, and seen through the haze of a summer's day, seems like a scene of fairyland."

The Wishing Stone, near the Beacon Mall, was blasted and taken away. Many a child, according to the superstition, has walked around it nine times and then, climbing to the top, would make a wish.

A great want, often expressed, was for a fountain and shrubbery.

The *United States Gazette* prints a series of letters entitled "A Trip to Boston" by Enoch Cobb Wines, who says: "In this cursory notice of some of the more striking features of Boston, it would be unpardonable to omit the 'Common,' as the public pleasure ground is here denominated. This is more than four times as large as any other similar place in the United States, embracing a little over fifty acres. It is enclosed by a fine iron railing, made in the most durable manner, and at an immense expense. Within and nearly contiguous, to this enclosure, there is a broad gravelled avenue, called the Mall. On one side of the Common this is shaded by three rows of lofty elms. The whole Common is thickly planted with trees of various kinds, most of them however, still young, and of course not yielding much shade. As nature in this region seems everywhere to have delighted in the line of beauty, the surface is broken into various knolls, and a small artificial lake near the center seems to diversify the scene. The great wants of this promenade are of fountains and shrubbery......

"Sallying forth with the intent and under the circumstances narrated in a previous communication, I first directed my steps toward the State House, and sought the prospect to be obtained from the top of its lofty dome. The view there revealed to the beholder would more than repay five times the present toil of the ascent. I would speak soberly and without exaggeration, and such I believe to be the declaration that there are few prospects either in the new world or the old, that can be compared with this. You know something of my title to speak in this manner, but I must vindicate it to others. Permit me, then, to say that I have had some opportunity of observation in various parts of the globe. I have stood upon the keep of Carisbrooke Castle in the Isle of Wight, on the Leaning Tower of Pisa, on the dome of the Cathedral at Florence, on the summits of Gibralter, Vesuvius, the Acro-Corinthus, and the Acropolis of Sardis, and on many other elevated points in all the four continents of Europe, Asia, Africa and America; and I declare to you that, to the best of my recollection, few of the prospects thus obtained are equal and fewer still superior, to that enjoyed from the State House at Boston."*

1839 NOVEMBER 19.

A new iron fence was finished around the cemetery on the Common.

The Public Garden began when its lands were laid out.

The Botanic Garden (on the site of the Public Garden), was started by a number of citizens, including Horace Gray. The conditions of the grant were that no buildings,—except a greenhouse and tool house—should be erected on the grounds. The large building, once used by a circus—corner of Charles and Beacon Streets, was turned into a conservatory where were displayed a fine collection of plants, and native and foreign singing birds. The building was destroyed by fire in a few years.

---

*Foot Note: "I am told that an artist is employed in making a panorama of Boston from this point. I did not learn. If it is well executed and true to the original, it will be a picture worth seeing.

1840 APRIL 19, 6 P. M.

Hawthorne in "American Note Books," says, "I went out to walk about an hour ago, and found it very pleasant, though there was a somewhat cool wind. I went round and across the Common, and stood on the highest point of it, where I could see miles and miles into the country. Blessed be God for this green tract, and the view which it affords, whereby we poor citizens may be put in mind, sometimes, that all his earth is not composed of blocks of brick houses, and of stone or wooden pavements. Blessed be God for the sky too, though the smoke of the city may somewhat change its aspect,—but still it is better than if each street were covered with a roof. There were a good many people walking on the Mall—mechanics apparently, and shopkeepers' clerks, with their wives; and boys were rolling on the grass, and I would have liked to lie down and roll too."

JULY 4.

A log cabin was erected as a political emblem on the Common.

JULY 4.

The new iron fence, extending between the Granary Burying Ground and Tremont Street, was finished.

The oldest stone in the Granary Burying Ground is located west of the Franklin monument. The inscription reads, "Here lies ye body of John Wakefield, aged 52 years, dec'd June ye 18th, 1667."

The oldest horizontal slab, as well as the first poetical epitaph, marks the grave of Mrs. Hannah Allen, wife of Rev. James Allen, pastor of the First Church, who died February 26, 1776.

"Stay thou, this grave that passeth by,
And think how soon that thou may'st dye;
If sex, or age, or virtue bright
Would have prolonged to thee it might,
Though virtue made not death to stay,
Yet turned it was to be their way,
And if with them thou would'st be blest,
Prepare to dye before thou rest."

LETTERS FROM NEW YORK.

By L. Maria Child (1852).

1841 August 21.

"I admit that Boston in her extensive and airy Common, possesses a blessing unrivalled by any other city; but I am not the less disposed to be thankful for the circumscribed, but well shaded, limits of the Washington Parade Grounds, and Union Park, with its nicely trimmed circle of hedge, its well-rolled gravel walks, and its velvet greensward, shaven as smooth as a Quaker beau." (Vol. 1, Letter 11, pp. 18.)

1841 Winter.

The boys skated on the Frog Pond which they called Quincy Lake.

April 21.

Funeral honors for the death of President Harrison caused great crowds to assemble on the sidewalks and on the Common.

APRIL 21.

The death of President Harrison was commemorated by an immense procession. The Lancers, Infantry and Artillery all formed on the Common when "even the heavens seemed to contribute their share of the solemn feelings of the day." The *Atlas,* of the 22nd, says: "The Mall along Beacon Street was lined with scholars of the various schools, with their teachers,—the girls being on the upper and the boys on the lower side."

OCTOBER.

Boston was "thrown into a most unusual state of excitement by the arrival of Lord Morpeth" who was *feted* by Charles Sumner and who was "afterward Earl of Carlisle and Lord Lieutenant of Ireland. He visited the Common.

NOVEMBER 24.

Prince De Joinville made a second visit to Boston and the Common.

Three houses remain which have stood more than sixty years; the Hancock House, the house at the bottom of the Mall, on Tremont Street, formerly owned by William Powell and now belonging to the heirs of William Foster, and a wooden building opposite the burying ground. They are seen from the centre of the Common.

The Park Street church occupies the location of the old Granary on the Common.

The principal schools, running back many years, were Proctor's (afterwards Carter's) School on Pemberton's

Hill; Tileston's in North School Street; Holbrook's in West Street, Paine's at the foot of (what is now), Morton Place, and the Latin School, under Master Lovell. Boys from all these schools played on the Common.

The Horse Pond on the Common, is filled up and the grass grown.

1842 JANUARY 22.

Dickens', in American Notes, says:—

Boston,—"When I got into the streets upon this Sunday morning the air was so clear, the houses were so bright and gay; the sign-boards were painted in such gaudy colors; the gilded letters were so very golden; the bricks were so very red; the stone was so very white, the blinds and area railings were so very green, the knobs and plates upon the street doors so marvelously bright and twinkling, and all so slight and unsubstantial in appearance—that every thoroughfare in the city looked exactly like a scene in a pantomine......

"The State House is built upon a summit of a hill, which rises gradually at first, and afterwards by a steep ascent, almost from the water's edge. In front is a green enclosure, called the Common. The site is beautiful and from the top there is a charming panoramic view of the whole town and neighborhood."

During the visit of Dickens to Boston many beautiful young ladies residing in the elegant mansions, would surround the great novelist and playfully cut small pieces of fur from his seal skin overcoat, which they kept as *souvenirs*.

February 1.

Dickens had a reception at Papant's Hall and visited the Common.

July 4.

Eight thousand school children were said to have been on the Common where 100,000 persons saw the fireworks in the evening.

July 27.

There was a Brigade-muster on the Common when fourteen companies came from Boston.

October 2.

Buckingham's America (London) Vol. 1, says, "Entered Boston. . . . . .The day was devoted to a review of the volunteer companies of the military of Boston, and as the weather was particularly fine, I went in the afternoon to the Common, where their exercises were conducted. This place for the number of men under arms was more favorable for display than either Hyde Park in London, or the Champs de Mars in Paris. The gently ascending slope of the ground, the fine grass, the surrounding avenues of trees, and the noble State House or Capitol, towering over the whole, with the fine ranges of buildings in Beacon Street, Park Street and Colonnade Row, on three of its sides, and an open view of the sea and one of the bridges leading to the suburbs on the fourth, made up a beautiful picture."

Children sailing boats on the Pond and watching their arrival on the opposite shore, also nurses with wicker carriages, were pleasant sights on the Common.

The homes of the wealthy on Park and Beacon Streets, derive great advantage by their view of the Common.

Church bells, calling people to worship at the Park Street Meeting house, caused many to walk across the Common.

Laborers combing grass with their rakes on the Common, in the spring.

Many played on the Common who now sleep on its border.

Land was offered for seventy-five cents a foot at the bottom of the Common and the land at the corner of Boylston and Tremont Streets—where the Masonic Temple now stands—at one dollar a foot, and, which, over thirty years afterwards could not be bought for ten dollars a foot. It was said at first that the land would never be any higher.

The brick sidewalk, around the Common, is a fashionable promenade and is even preferred to the Mall with its row of shade trees.

It was proposed that the water dropping from the top of the State House be utilized into a fountain in the centre of the Frog Pond on the Common. The plan failed.

The *Boston Miscellany* contains an engraving by Hammatt Billings, of the "Boston Common."

1843 MAY.

The Ghingo was planted on the east side of the Common.

JULY.

5319 visitors ascended to the top of the State House cupola for the view of the Common and the surrounding country.

SEPTEMBER 4.

General Winfield Scott visited Boston and the Common.

SEPTEMBER 20.

Macready, in his "Reminiscences," again says: "The mate summoned me at early twilight with the news that we should soon approach the 'Boston Harbour Light'... with the clustered masses of the city's buildings in the central distance, surrounded by the dome of the State House and the obelisk of Bunker Hill."

OCTOBER 12.

Richard M. Johnson (Tecumseh) visited Boston and the Common.

The Gun House, on the Common, was removed to near Park Square.

1844 MAY 10.

A company of volunteers, comprising seventy-five men and officers, came from Vermont and encamped on the Common on their way to the Mexican war.

MAY.

Trees were planted on the east side of the Common.

JULY 4.

The last display of fireworks occurred on the easterly side of the Common.

SEPTEMBER 19.

The Whig Convention—10,000 persons assembled on the Common. The *Boston Daily Bee* says,—

"The procession got back on the Common about two o'clock, when the Convention was called to order by Hon. Daniel Webster, the President of the meeting, who then made a short address......Great enthusiasm prevailed throughout the afternoon and the Convention adjourned at half-past five, to meet again by torch light, on the Common, in the evening."

America and the American people — by Frederick Von Raumer, Professor of History in the University of Berlin says,—

"BOSTON, SEPTEMBER 20.

Yesterday we passed a day peculiarly American; there being here a 'mass meeting of the Whigs.' The time from nine till one was spent by the companies in putting themselves in order, and marching in procession through many parts of the city, where a stage had been erected for the orator of the day. The streets were ornamented with numerous banners, pieces of tapestry, and emblematic devices, and the windows were filled with ladies, who testified their approbation by waving their handkerchiefs. Hurrahs resounded in every direction; but they were briefer and more moderate than those of the South. A large number of well mounted horsemen were followed by the procession on foot, in regular divisions, consisting of citizens of Boston and strangers present on the occasion. Many of the banners and legends were not wanting in wit and significance, although the opposite party could easily attach to some of them a contrary meaning. The standard of Maine, for instance when the loco-focos are in the majority bore the inscription, 'Wait till November!' For Tennessee there was only *one* man present; and the motto was, 'Tennessee is doing her duty at home.' A large strong carriage contained a number of young girls dressed in blue and white, and waving flags which bore the names of the different states. Two carriages succeeded each other filled with mechanics; one of which bore the inscription, 'Henry Clay and Frelinghuysen; protective duties for American industry,' and the other, 'Polk and Dallas, Free Trade.' The former carriage was a handsome one, the driver and working men well dressed, the horses in excellent condition, etc., the latter was the reverse in every particular. The last in the procession carried a banner inscribed 'Millions are behind us!'......It bespeaks much previous training and admirable bringing up, that so vast a number of men can associate without disorder, and without the direction or supervision of soldiers and policemen."

The "Whig Mass Meeting on Boston Common, September 19, 1844" drawn by ——— Sheldon, Jr., and lithographed by Thayer & Co., Boston, shows the State House dome and the church steeple, while "Old Glory" waves from three flagstaffs.

Plans for Beautifying and Enlarging Boston—by Robert Gourlay Fleming, says: "Most fortunately, the Common was at an early day devoted to the health and recreation of citizens of Boston, and mercifully was the Botanic Garden withheld for building on, as once contemplated."

1845 APRIL 10.

Deacon Samuel H. Hewes, Superintendent of Burials—died. He had planted 172 trees on the Common.

JULY 4.

The first display of fireworks on the Parade Ground occurred on the Common.

Local Loiterings and Visits in the Vicinity of Boston —by "A Looker On," (John Dix Ross) says, "As I was strolling through the leafy arcades of Boston Common a few evenings since, and watching with curious and pleased eyes the throngs who passed me by, my fancy took unto herself wings and flew away to the times when a former generation paraded there—when the noble trees, which now form such natural and graceful arches overhead, roofing the broad aisles with their masses of foliage, through which the flickering sunbeams paved the walks with a kind of mosaic gold, were young, or newly planted—and when many, whose names are yet familiar, sauntered there in all the pride of youth and beauty......

"And let us take a bird's-eye view of the Common, and for that purpose we will ascend to the dome of the State House, which looms up like a little Saint Paul's. Stay—and before we mount let us admire the statue of Washington, by Chantrey; the philosopher, statesman and soldier delineated by the great sculptor......

"I have witnessed a number of what are called very

fine sights in my time—I have been present at the Queen's Coronation, and at other such imposing spectacles, but I can in all sincerity, aver that none ever yielded me so much pleasure as the view on Boston Common on the evening of the recent Fourth of July. ...... The sun was rapidly sinking as I passed through the gates and mixed with the multitude, who passed on towards the spot where the fireworks were to be exhibited. And as I stood on the eminence, near the Pond, what a magnificent sight met my gaze!

"A happy name is that—Boston Common! There is nothing exclusive about it, and the term emphatically implies that it is, what it indeed *is,* common as the breezes which sweep along its surface, and the sky which smiles above it. It is the great Lung to the throbbing city-heart, and the organ in which the renovating and healing influences are to be found—a place where care may be for a while banished, and in which anxiety may smooth his ruffled brow. It is alike a resort of youth and age—for the frivolist and the philosopher. Innocence may sport there without soiling its beautiful garments —and then the grief that comes with years may find solace and relief. Fortunate was Boston in having had far sighted men for its founders, and doubly fortunate are those, who can with pride remember the wisdom of their ancestors, as they realize the enjoyments which, in the benevolence of their hearts, they planned."

Among the residents of Summer Street, and the surrounding neighborhood, who were often seen walking on the Common, were, Jacob Sleeper, Isaac Rich, Lee Claflin, Nathaniel Goddard, James Jackson, William R. Gray, Horace Gray, John Welles, Dr. Alexander

Young, Rev. Francis William Pitt, Dr. Orville Dewey, both of the New South Church—Rufus Choate, Edward Everett, Daniel Webster, Colonel Sever, William Parsons, Benjamin Loring, James C. Paige, Captain Sturgis, Henry Gassett, Henry Higginson, Benjamin Rich, Charles Brooks, William Rollins, Alexander H. Everett, Israel Thorndike, George Blake, John Tappan, Benjamin Bussey, John P. Cushing, Drs. John Sylvester Gardiner, Jonathan Mayhew, Franklin Dexter, Dr. E. H. Robbins and also Marion Weston Chapman who earnestly advocated the cause of abolition.

Winthrop Place: Thomas H. Perkins, Jr., William H. Gardiner, Isaac MacLellan, Isaac P. Davis, Benjamin A Gould, father of the astronomer of the same name—George Bond, H. Hollis Hunnewell, Thomas Motley, Henry Cabot, John E. Lodge, George Bancroft, Samuel Cabot, Joshua Blake, Francis Staunton, Thomas Lamb, Josiah Parsons Cooke and Samuel Greele.

Otis Place: Nathaniel Bowditch, Bryant P. Tilden, Samuel G. Williams, Oliver Eldredge, Augustus Thorndike, Jeremiah S. Boies, Charles Thorndike, Richard D. Tucker, Eben Rollins and John L. Gardner.

JULY 9.

Funeral honors for the death of General Jackson drew great crowds to the streets and Common.

NOVEMBER 17.

The Winthrop House was opened. Many guests went down to the Common.

Parade grounds prepared on the west side of the Common.

1846 MAY 1.

The *Boston Daily Journal* makes the following announcement: "Artillery election: A promenade concert and children's dance is to come off at the Public Gardens on Monday afternoon, provided the weather is favorable. Bouquets will be offered for sale. An excellent band of music will be stationed on the grounds."

AUGUST 25, FIVE O'CLOCK A. M.

A slight shock of earthquake was felt on the Common.

SEPTEMBER 21.

The Adams House was formally opened. Its patrons often came to the Common.

1847 MAY 1.

The Revere House, on Bowdoin Square, was completed and opened when many went to the Common.

JUNE 9.

Some mischievous boys played a trick by trying to burn the "Old Elm" by igniting matches and throwing them into a decayed place.

JUNE 29.

President Polk visited Boston and was greeted with a warm reception while many were on the Common.

JULY 27.

New iron seats were placed on the Common. They prevented whittling.

AUGUST 2.

The removal of buildings on the Common.

The *Boston Daily Journal,* says: The small buildings are marching off the Training Field and the brick engine and school house, so to speak, are preparing to follow. The school house is to take a sort of right wheel, and back down in the lot lately purchased, fronting the Training Field on Common Street. It is a huge undertaking to move so large a brick building, but we presume it can be done with perfect safety by the contractors.

NOVEMBER 20.

The cornerstone of the Beacon Hill Reservoir was laid when many witnessed the ceremonies on the Common.

The cornerstone of the Boston Athenaeum, on Beacon Street, was laid, which brought many to the Common.

1848 JANUARY 7.

$1100 was found and recovered, by Marshall Tukey, by digging in the Public Garden.

FEBRUARY 23.

John Quincy Adams died in Washington. Funeral obsequies were held in Boston when the "black coffin" was seen by the crowds on the streets as the procession slowly passed to the music of the Dead March. Many assembled on the Common.

MARCH 14.

General Sam Houston lectured at Tremont Temple and visited the Common.

AUGUST.

The bottom of the Frog Pond, on the Common, was paved with stones.

OCTOBER 25.

Cochituate water was introduced in Boston when the Frog Pond (called "Crescent" since the building of the wall) was used as an illustrator in the celebration and became "Fountain Pond" by the new and beautiful fountain.

OCTOBER 25.

The Cochituate water celebration was a memorable event. A vast parade proceeded through the different streets and ended on the Common where a platform—occupied by Mayor Quincy and other distinguished citizens—was built over the Frog Pond. Fountain streams, turned on, rose high in the air as school children sang "My name is Water" amid the ringing of bells and the sound of cannon while rockets rose to the sky. At a dinner given by the Boston Latin School thirty-five years afterwards (1883) Hon. Robert S. Rantoul read a poem, recalling an incident of school boy days, in this event, containing the following stanza:

"Behold the stately pageant wind along the choking street!
From mart and house-top streaming flags our civic feast day greet!
By the dark Frog pond's mimic flood I see our cohorts drawn,
As, line on line, by Beacon Hill, they tramp the sloping lawn,
I feel October's eager air toy with each silken fold
Of that bright flag whose 'P. L. S.' our modest legend told.

I hear the bells, with clangorous tongue the waning day
ring out;
I watch the rockets' fiery trail—I catch the exultant
shout
That rolled—it seems but yester—e'en along the Park
Street crest
Just as the red Autumnal sun sank in the purple west,
From State House dome, down Flag Staff Hill, to lazy
Charles' banks,—
The wild huzza that scaled the sky from out those school-
boy ranks,
When from its base of molten bronze the crystal column
rose!
Long Pond, at last, by Blackstone's Spring in iron
arteries flows!
And Boston claims her destined bride, the fair Cochitu-
ate,
As Quincy turns the water on, in Eighteen Forty-eight!"

A "View of the Water Celebration on Boston Common, October 25, 1848," drawn on stone by Samuel W. Rowse from a sketch by B. F. Smith, Jr., and lithographed by Tappan and Bradford, Boston, shows the figures of Daniel Webster, Longfellow and others in the foreground.

October 25.

A long pond was opened, near the Frog Pond, on the Common.

October 25.

The Frog Pond was again improved and Cochituate water was drawn from a new hydrant.

OCTOBER 25.

The Liberty pole was removed to the big hill.

Flag staff removed from big elm to Flag Staff hill.

1849 FEBRUARY 28.

Chief Objewa was at Faneuil Hall and went to the Common.

SEPTEMBER 28.

A fountain was opened in front of the State House.

NOVEMBER 23.

The reservoir was completed on Beacon Hill.

"Frothingham's Seige of Boston," contains: "A plan of the Town of Boston, with the intrenchments, etc., of His Majesty's Forces in 1775, from the Observations of Lieut. Page of His Majesty's Corps of Engineers and from the Plans of other Gentlemen..... Engraved for William Faden, Charing Cross, as the Act directs, last October, 1777."

1850

Frederika Bremer, in Homes of the New World,—says: "Boston, February 1. I was pleased by (a) visit to the State House of Boston, which is also, in its exterior, a magnificent building. Two immense fountains cast up their waters in front of its facade, and from the flight of steps outside the house the view is splendid. Below lies the extensive green called 'Boston Common,' in the middle of which is also a beautiful fountain which throws up its water to a great height. Round it, on three sides, run three remarkably beautiful streets, each street planted through its whole length with lofty trees, mostly the elm, the favorite tree of Massachusetts, and some of the same kind beautify also the park-like Common. On the fourth side is an open view of the ocean creek. Here on the broad causeways, beneath the beautiful elms, I am fond of walking when the weather is mild, to behold through the branches of the trees the bright blue heaven of Massachusetts."

FEBRUARY 19.

A liberty block was completed on the spot of the Liberty Tree.

AUGUST 15.

Funeral obsequies for the death of President Taylor drew many people to the streets and Common.

DECEMBER 5.

Lieutenant Maury lectured at the Lowell Institute and visited the Common.

The Common, originally of much larger proportions, has been reduced in size, from time to time, until it was thought to be of the right proportion for the town.

One reads of Colonel T. H. Perkins, who, in an earlier generation, went snipe shooting on the Common.

Daniel Webster, like many Bostonians, walked, before breakfast, outside the Common, every morning, also Edward Everett and his son took the same walk. Rufus Choate once blended with his morning walk the study of German on the Common.

Sprague's Writings,—Boston; on the title page is an engraving of the "Old Elm."

A *common* occurrence furnishes a witticism.

1851 APRIL 3.

The capture of a runaway slave—Thomas Semmes caused much talk in town and on the Common.

MAY 3.

Gleason's Pictorial contains a picture—drawn by "J. H. M." of the "Anti-Slavery Meeting on the Common."

JUNE 3.

General John E. Wool visited the city and Common.

JUNE.

A Smokers Retreat, with seats, was started on the Common.

Gleason's Pictorial (Sept. 20) has a picture of the "Smokers Circle on Boston Common."

The Grand Railroad Jubilee "commemorative of the opening of communication between Boston and Canada lasted three days."

SEPTEMBER 17.

The first day: Lord Elgin, and other distinguished guests, were escorted to various points of interest in the city including the Common.

The second day: A large military procession marched from the City Hall, in School Street, through Tremont, Court, Cambridge, Chambers, Green and Pitt Streets, Haymarket Square, Blackstone, Clinton and

South Market Streets, Merchants Row, State, Washington, Dover and Tremont to the corner of Park where it entered the Common, where they were reviewed by President Fillmore, who sat in a barouche side of Mayor Bigelow, and passing long groups of merry children, on the Mall, went out the Boylston Street gate.

SEPTEMBER 19.

The third day: A grand dinner given to the guests visiting the city and attended by 3600 persons was spread in a Pavilion, erected on the end of the Common toward the Public Garden, where speeches were made by Lord Elgin, Governor Boutwell, Edward Everett, Robert C. Winthrop and others.

A grand display of fireworks came off in the evening.

Gleason's Pictorial (Nov. 15) has a sketch: a "Dinner Festival on Boston Common at the Railroad Jubilee." A motto over an (interior) archway reads: "Mercantile Enterprise, Railroad and Telegraph, Boston 1630 to 1851." Various flags wave on the ceiling.

A Court decision gave a title to the centre of a street when a question was asked if the same decision did not affect the public squares and the Common.

Much is being done to make the Common more attractive.

1852 APRIL 29.

Louis Kossuth came, lecturing at Faneuil Hall, and visited the Common.

OCTOBER 18.

The Board of Aldermen passed an order establishing the Parade Ground.

With Thackeray in America,—by Eyre Crowe, A. L. A. (1893) says, October, "We had overhead, a most glorious sunset effect of cloudland, quite eclipsing the now already darkening outline of the distant town of Boston......We bumped into Boston by circuitous routes, till we reached the hospitable shelter of the Tremont house. Visits were made on the 'poet Bunn' and Madame Sontag both of whom were at the Revere House......The claims then paramount of the Tremont and the Revere hotels have succumbed to those of yet more splendid ones, called the Vendome and the Brunswick." Of the Bunker Hill Monument, Mr. T. says: "I naturally went to inspect it, crossing the Charlestown Ferry for that purpose," and, viewing the outline of the city from that spot, he again says, (since the dedication of the monument), "probably ulterior conflagrations and demolitions may have quite altered its aspect since then." The Common was visited.

The charming work—John Lothrop Motley and his Family—Further letters and records—edited by his daughter and Herbert St. John Mildmay (1910) says in a letter:

"From Mrs. Thomas Motley to J. L. M."

NOVEMBER 11.

"Sontag who is now singing in Boston......

"I have heard her once, and I shall hear her again tomorrow. I cannot pretend to criticise her, but she filled me with delight; such a pure sweet voice, such exquisite whispered melody, I never heard; not the faintest tone is lost, but as distinct as her fullest notes. Her toilette is exquisite as is her grace, and she is so pretty......I hear that she will not sing here again; she dreads the climate so much. Unfortunately the new music hall is not quite finished. She sang at the Melodeon which was filled full, and the applause was unbounded. She was finely supported. The Germani, Bacchial, Jacel and the wonderful little violinist Paul Julian, several other singers who, I believe, are in her suite, Pozzolini, Rocco, etc., I do not think you can compare her with others; her voice has not the wonderful power of Jenny Lind, but she has so much more grace and beauty and she makes up in sweetness and finish for the passion of the Italian." She visited the Common.

NOVEMBER 30.

Great funeral ceremonies in honor of Daniel Webster were held in Boston at the close of which many persons went to the Common.

1853 MARCH 23.

The Light Dragoons were organized and paraded on the Common.

SEPTEMBER 8.

The west end addition of the State House was completed.

NOVEMBER.

The lands of the Public Garden were again offered for sale.

Charles Mackay wrote one of his poems of nature of which, it is said, he was "prompted thereto by the sight of some daisies growing on Boston Common!" Perchance it may have been "A Reverie in the Grass" containing the lines:

"Here let me rest, amid the bearded grass,
Sprinkled with buttercups, and idly pass
One hour of sunshine on the green hill slope;
Watching the rigid clouds, that o'er the cope
Of visible heaven sail quietly along;
Listening the wind, or rustling leaves, or song
Of blackbird, or sweet ring dove in the copse
Of pines and sycamores, whose dark green tops
Form a clear outline right against the blue
Here let me lie and dream."

1854 MAY 24.

Anthony Burns, a fugitive slave, was arrested in Boston, Theodore Parker, Samuel G. Howe, and Thomas Wentworth Higginson called a meeting in Faneuil Hall where loud expressions of indignation were poured forth to a vast audience. An attack was made on the Court House where the negro was confined, but which was repelled by the police. Burns, surrounded by the military, was led through the streets, while the bells rang and amid the hoots and jeers of the crowd, to the end of Long Wharf and sent back to the South. Sympathy for the unfortunate negro was expressed on the streets and on the Common.

JULY 4.

Balloon ascensions were of frequent occurrence on the Common.

AUGUST 23.

Five men were killed by a shell explosion on the Common.

The gate of the iron fence around the "Old Elm"

bears the inscription, "This tree has been standing here for an unknown period. It is believed to have existed before the settlement of Boston, being full grown in 1722, exhibited marks of old age in 1792, and was nearly destroyed by a storm in 1832. Protected by an iron enclosure in 1854. J. V. C. Smith, Mayor."

1855 AUGUST 3.

The box containing the remains of Major General Joseph Warren, which were taken from the Granary Burying Ground to St. Paul's Church, (1825) were buried in Forest Hills Cemetery.

SEPTEMBER 17.

Laying of the corner stone of the Public Library on Boylston Street. Many went to the Common.

The "Old Elm" is venerated as a relic of the Indian Shawmut.

It was considered probable that, from its growth and size, the "Old Elm" was 200 years old.

The "Old Elm" is regarded as "one of the finest natural ornaments in this part of the country."

The State House was enlarged and a new corner stone laid, the Grand Lodge of Massachusetts having charge of the ceremonies which drew a great crowd to the Common.

Theodore Parker who preached to multitudes in Boston Music Hall, Thomas Starr King whose powerful voice was heard in the Hollis Street Church, Channing whose magic tones are ever remembered, Father Taylor who preached to sailors in his Bethel, Gough whose imitations of victims of intemperance thrilled many an audience, Julius Booth the unrivalled tragedian were all seen walking on the Common.

1856 FEBRUARY 23.

Ballou's Pictorial contains a "Snow Scene on Boston Common."

JUNE.

Bodies were removed from the north side of the Neck to prepare for a hotel site.

AUGUST 16.

Ballou's Pictorial contains an engraving of a "Promenade Concert on Boston Common."

SEPTEMBER 17.

The Inauguration of the Statue of Franklin. The parade of the Fire Department was one of the features of the procession. At three o'clock in the afternoon, at the close of the procession, they proceeded to the westerly end of the Common where an exhibition of throwing water was witnessed by thousands of spectators.

At the Inauguration ceremonies of the Franklin Statue, among the many congratulatory letters sent, by the mayors of various cities, to the mayor of Boston, was the following:

Pittsfield, September 17.

To His Honor the Mayor of Boston.

You do us honor over much. We are a rural town as yet, without a mayor; but the "Old Elm" of Pittsfield sends greetings; to the "Old Elm" of Boston Common, and to his honor the Mayor of Boston, while the western border of Massachusetts claims her share in the glory which Franklin shed over the old Commonwealth, and finds his illustrious birthplace and his new statue.

The Old Elm of Pittsfield."

1858 JANUARY 1.

The dedication of the Boston Public Library occurred when 1500 persons assembled at the City Hall, at half-past three o'clock and formed in procession, escorted by the Boston Light Infantry headed by the Boston Band, and marched through School, Beacon, Park, to the new library building on Boylston Street where, with exercises and music, the keys were delivered to Mayor Rice. Many strolling on the Common.

MONDAY, JULY 5.

(The Fourth occurring on Sunday), the Eighty-second anniversary of American Independence—a mild, clear day—crowds assembled on the Common and Parks awaiting the events of the day. Bells rang at sunrise and cannon pealed forth from different quarters of the city. One of the features was the "Brass Concert" on the Common where 50,000 persons listened to

(1) Hail Columbia
(2) Yankee Doodle
(3) Woodup
(4) Washington's March
(5) The Anvil Chorus
(6) The Star Spangled Banner
(7) God Save the Queen
(8) La Marseillaise

(9) The Russian National Hymn
(10) The Turkish March.

The "Young America's Frolic" at the Public Garden added pleasure to the juveniles who passed the time in singing, dancing, etc., as the Germania Band played sweet music with exhibitions of cameras obscuros, mammoth kaleidoscopes, etc. The day opened by fancy dances and at noon the song, written by T. W. Parsons, was sung resounding through the trees. An oration was delivered by John S. Holmes, before a large audience at Music Hall. The "City Dinner" took place at Faneuil Hall where addresses were made by Mayor Lincoln, Governor Banks, Mr. Everett, Judge Sanger, Mr. A. A. Lawrence, Mr. Joseph Howe, and Rev. S. K. Lothrop.

The Democratic celebration was held in Tremont Temple where the orator was Rufus Choate and followed by a Banquet at the Revere House in the afternoon, where speeches were made by Mr. Williamson, Mr. Everett, Mr. Austin, Mr. Hallet, Mr. Webster, Mr. Woodbury, Mr. Davis, General Palfrey, Governor Stevens, and Mayor Lincoln.

On the Common a grand balloon ascension drew a great crowd as the Ganymede with Mr. Charles E. Wise arose, at four o'clock in the afternoon, and descended at Malden Centre, before six, creating much curiosity. At half-past five another balloon Jupiter—in care of the elder Mr. Wise, with Mr. S. C. Burr and Mr. Lyman, W. Brittan—ascended, and lost to view in ten minutes, came down at Melrose, at half-past seven o'clock. A grand display of fireworks was witnessed on the Common in the evening.

October 11.

Jefferson Davis came to Boston and visited the Common.

The Old Blue Ball—an old landmark—that had stood for over two centuries with an old sign suspended on the corner of Union and Hanover Streets, the site of the residence of Josiah Franklin, was demolished. Many loitering out often went to the Common.

Oliver Wendell Holmes, in the Autocrat of the Breakfast Table, is said to have made immortal the "Long Path," running from Joy to Boylston Street, on the Common.

An amusing custom with certain boys was to bury an old trunk, containing several dollars in coin, at the beginning of the present Commonwealth Avenue, at the side of the Public Garden. The plot, however, was discovered as in one of the searches the trunk had already disappeared.

1859 January 19.

Edward Everett, in an address, entitled "Franklin the Boston Boy," delivered before the Association of Franklin Medal Scholars in Music Hall, said of the Old Granary Burying Ground, where the parents of Franklin lie buried, that it now lays in the centre of the population of the city and was formerly on the outskirts of the town, and is now surrounded by the Tremont House, the Park Street Church, the Boston Athenaeum and some of the costliest homes of the city in Park and Beacon Streets. The front of the cemetery is shaded by a row of eleven majestic English Elms planted by Major Adino Paddock and John Ballard, nearly a century ago.

April 1.

A startling announcement was made in the Boston papers that a cave was discovered, which drew many persons to the Parade Ground near the Boylston Street end of the Common, who paid a small fee to enter the canvas covering, but before the close of the day everyone learned that they had been *April fooled.*

July 4.

A morning band concert on the Common.

Ballou's Pictorial (July) has a "Fourth of July scene on Boston Common."

July 7.

An elephant, belonging to Sam Rice, bathed in the Frog Pond on the Common.

August 15.

A military company from Montreal drilled on the Common.

September 17.

A statue of Webster was placed in front of the State House.

October.

Foot ball was often played, on the Common, and a match game occurred between Dixwell's private Latin School and the Boston Public Latin School. The opposing goals were the Beacon Street Mall and the path leading from Flagstaff Hill to Charles Street.

On the extension of Back Bay, George H. Snelling petitioned the Legislature that the plan of the Commissioners be so modified that, instead of the houses and lots on Commonwealth Avenue, a broad basin of water should run east and west, and thus permitting the south west winds, in summer, to blow, as before, over the open space. The plan was approved by certain newspapers and citizens, and a letter from Charles Sumner, thanked Mr. Snelling for his "timely intervention to save our Boston Common by keeping it open to the western breezes and to the setting sun." The plan, however, remained unaltered.

The game of hockey was very popular, sides were each day formed on the Parade Ground on the Common.

When the Parade Ground was filled in at the end of Boylston Street, hundreds of loads of oyster shells were used for dumping purposes which were often made missels of and sent "flying through the air."

A Boston boy relates how he once batted a ball high up among the green leaves of the trees on the Beacon Street Mall where it passed out of sight and was never seen, or heard of, again.

The old hand engines were: *Mazeppa* No. 1, *Perkins* No. 2, *Eagle* No. 3, *Cataract* No. 4, *Extinguisher* No. 5, *Melville* No. 6, *Tiger* No. 7, *Boston* No. 8, *Maverick* No. 9, *Dunbar* No. 10, *Barnicoat* No. 11, *Tremont* No. 12, etc., etc. Five or more, of these companies often met for a rival test to determine which could throw the highest stream on the Common.

A West End negro and a *South Ender*—between whom trouble existed—met on the Common where, after loud, angry words, the negro threw a stone, which he held in his hand, at the head of his antagonist causing severe injuries.

Flag Staff Hill was a popular coasting ground.

Many citizens made kites for their children, which were raised on the Common. Dr. Nathaniel B. Shurtleff — once Mayor of Boston — excelled in making Chinese kites resembling owls with glaring eyes.

Tipcat (chasing a cat with a twisted willow stick), was a popular game on the Common.

Cricket had grown to be a favorite game; and a number of clubs were formed, viz.: the "Boston," the "Bay State," the "Glen and Thistle," the "Young Bostons," the "Mount Vernon," etc., but, who, finding the ground of the Common too hard to place a wicket, or bowling crease, went to grounds at East Cambridge.

Among the boys who played on the Common were: Henry Cabot Lodge, William Walley, Samuel Cabot, Arthur Brooks, George Lyman, Charlie and Rollins Morse, George Mifflin, Cabot Russell, Sam and Gus. Bradstreet, Arthur Beebe, Henry and Joe Fay, Billy Field, Lem Stanwood, "Ren" Thayer, Ned Burgess, Malcolm Greenough, Frank Manning, Frank Nicholson, Tom Motley, etc., etc. One of their achievements was to vault over the pickets of the iron fence.

Charles Mackay, in Life and Liberty in America,

says, "Boston the capital of the small but ancient, wealthy, and intelligent commonwealth of Massachusetts, the model and most conservative state of the Union, is one of the most picturesque as well as important cities of America. The original Indian name of the small peninsula on which it is built was 'Shawmut' or the 'Living Fountains.' From the three hills on which it stands, which have been now partly levelled, it obtained from the early settlers the name of Tremont, or Tri-mountain—a name still given to it by poets and orators, when they strive to be particularly eloquent.... The old city, or Boston proper, stands on a peninsula, surrounded by salt water on three sides, and on the fourth by the brackish water of the Charles River, which at its confluence with the sea, spreads out like a small lake. It is connected by a narrow strip of land, not more than two feet above high water, and called the Neck, with the suburb or city of Roxbury......The great charm of the Scenery of Boston is its Common or Park—a piece of ground covering about forty acres, and open on one side to the Charles River, over the estuary of which, and the heights beyond, it commands from every part a series of extensive and beautiful views. The other sides of the Common are occupied by the residences of the principal inhabitants—noble stone buildings most of them—and representing a rental ranging from £300 to £800 or £1000 per annum. House rent is exceedingly high in all the great American cities, and is at least double that of houses of the corresponding style in London. In all distant views the State House dominates the city as the highest and most conspicuous object, around which everything else is concentrated. The view from the top of this edifice well repays the labor of the ascent and affords an unrivalled panorama of the busy, populous, and charming home which the descendants of the ancient English Puritans have made for themselves in the New World. In the Common, surrounded by a railing to protect it from injury, stands a venerable elm, with an inscription stating that it is believed to have been planted before the first settlement of Boston as a colony, and that it began to exhibit signs of old age a quarter of a century ago. Its boughs are inhabited by a colony of tame gray squirrels. To throw nuts to these graceful little creatures, and watch their gambols, is one of the principal amusements of the nurse maids, and children of Boston, as well as of many older and wiser persons. There are similar colonies in the other elms in some of the principal streets. The squirrels are general favorites, and have no enemies except among the cats, which occasionally make an inroad upon them and diminish their numbers, to the great disgust and indignation of the well-minded population. It may be mentioned as an interesting fact in natural history that the elms in Boston planted by the English settlers from slips or seeds brought from England retain their leaves much later than the native American elms. At this advanced period of the year may be noticed, amid the leafless or the brown and yellow trees that grace the Common, seven elms of most luxuriant green foliage which seem not to have lost a leaf, or to possess a leaf in the slightest degree discolored. There are the English elms, sturdy Britons, flourishing vigorously, while their Yankee brethren seedy, sapless, and wo-begone, look as sallow as if they too, like their human compatriots, smoked immoderately, chewed tobacco, spat, lived in heated rooms, and, in their over-eagerness to get rich, did injustice to their physical nature."

Messrs. Ticknor and Fields bookstore, on Washington Street, well known throughout the country has long been a literary *arena* for scholars and authors. Many of the brightest stars in literature have been seen there. Longfellow the dearly loved poet, Professor Agassiz who endeared himself to the scholarly world by his words that "he had no time to make money" and whose love of American institutions made him refuse an offer of Napoleon III to go to Paris; Oliver Wendell Holmes who excelled in sparkling wit, Prescott the historian, besides poets, Clergymen, writers, journalists, editors, professors, scholars, poetessės, students, matrons, etc., etc., who have there met and dicussed the merits of new books. The *aesthetic* air of Boston, with the Common, has gained it the name of being the "Athens of the New World," though New York, Philadelphia, and other cities of the United States claim equal social and literary distinction.

An act for the acceptance of the Public Garden was passed and flower beds and paths were laid out.

A Ferris wheel, that rose to the heighth of 40 or 50 feet, was erected and a smaller one for the less venturesome.

In winter the pond was as popular for skaters as the Frog Pond on the Common.

The Public Garden was the camping ground for all the circuses of an earlier day that came to Boston.

The Public Garden is surrounded by busy streets, substantial office buildings, stores, churches, theatres, hotels, club houses, and costly residences. The State House stands on an eminence on Beacon Street while the harbor is a mile eastward.

1860 May 16.

A vote to cut the trees down on Paddock's Mall was carried.

June 29, at half-past six p. m.

The "Old Elm" was seriously injured in a storm, the loss of a large branch, that fell, ruined its natural beauty.

October 17.

The Prince of Wales was tendered a reception in Boston with a military review on the Common.

The ruins of a fort, built by the British in 1775, could be seen on the Common. It stood, with mounted cannon, south of the Frog Pond, overlooking the town.

A great gale did not injure the trees on the Common.

We speak of the Boston of Edward Everett, Louise Chandler Moulton, Cooper, Bynner, Lydia Maria Child, Emerson, Thoreau, Hawthorne, Longfellow, Lowell, Holmes, Ticknor, Motley, Prescott, Parker, Whittier, Sumner, Agassiz, Howells, Whipple, Aldrich, Phillips Brooks, Edward Everett Hale, Horace Mann, Julia Ward Howe, Burlingame, Andrew, Wilson, Hoar, Alcott, James Freeman Clarke, George H. Hepworth, William R. Alger, Savage, George Ripley, Osgood Parkman, etc., all of whom have frequently walked on the Common.

The charming biography—Louise Chandler Moulton, Poet and Friend—by Lillian Whiting (1910) says: "Mrs. Spofford, writing of Mrs. Moulton from personal memory, says of her in 1860: 'She was now in her twenty-fifth year, fully launched upon the literary high-seas, contributing to *Harpers,* the *Galaxy,* and *Scribner's* as they came into existence, and to the *Young Folks,* the *Youth's Companion* and other periodicals for children. Her life seemed a fortunate one. She had a charming home in Boston where she met and entertained the most pleasant people.....The intellectual and the social were closely blended in the Boston of the sixties and the seventies, and Mrs. Moulton was in the very midst of the most characteristically Bostonian circles.' "

The dwellings that surround the Common excel in elegance and comfort. Those on Park Street have a highly picturesque view.

Probably no place is more cherished by those who, in childhood, trundled hoops or played ball, marbles, etc., besides the many sights, seen on the Common.

Great improvements were made, in the Public Garden, by the city.

Policemen patrolling the Common were so frequently asked to point out the favorite seat of Lemuel Barker that they all agreed upon one, but which, perchance, may have admitted of as much doubt as many of the bullets said to have been picked up on the field of Waterloo.

THE CIVIL WAR

1861

APRIL 17.

Governor Andrew, the war governor, presented a set of colors to the Sixth Massachusetts Regiment—Colonel Edward F. Jones—on their departure for Washington. The presentation address was made from the steps of the State House while the troops were drawn up in line, on Beacon Street, causing a great crowd to gather on the Common.

APRIL 19.

The Eighth Regiment, en route to the war, passed through Boston when the Common was well filled.

JUNE 3.

The First Marine Regiment passed through Boston and was seen by many on the streets and Common.

JUNE 15.

The First Massachusetts Regiment—the first three years regiment to depart for the war—leaving camp Cameron (in North Cambridge), marched to the Common where they were greeted by wives, parents, sweethearts and friends on the Parade Grounds, which, roped off, could only be entered, by the great crowd, on the Charles Street side. The day was hot and sultry and the men, wearing their overcoats, were greatly exhausted when they reached their destination. The Regimental historian, writes: "The line swayed to and fro a few moments, and then, over the rope, in every direction; the earnest and excited mass of humanity plunged; and much more speedily than it takes to write it, officers, soldiers, and civilians were mixed up in one immense throng of people, weeping, laughing, embracing, clinging to one another, and presenting here and there scenes so affecting, that the recollection of them is as fresh and vivid today as on the evening when they transpired." When the regiment departed only two-thirds marched in "regular order," the rest followed, in the midst of the people, to the Providence Depot where they became the recipients of a beautiful banner which it was intended to present them on the Common, but which was prevented by the crowds.

JULY 8.

The Second Regiment left for the war causing many to go to the Common.

JULY 18.

The Twelfth Regiment, commanded by Fletcher Webster, a son of the distinguished New Hampshire statesman, was presented with a handsome set of colors on the Common. The address was delivered by Hon. Edward Everett while the city donated a collation which was spread under the trees on the Beacon Street Mall.

The song "John Brown's body lies mouldering in the grave," is said to have first been sung by "The Tigers" of the Twelfth Regiment on the Common.

"My Country, 'tis of thee" in the Park Street Church.

JULY 19.

The arrival of the Fourth Regiment, from the war, caused a great number to go to the Common.

July 25.

The departure of the Tenth Regiment for the war caused great crowds on the Common.

July.

The Third and Fourth Regiments (23d) and the Fifth (30th) and the Sixth (Aug. 1), were welcomed back and sat to a "bountiful collation" on the Beacon Street Mall. Many of the men re-enlisted. The *Advertiser* (Aug. 2), says of the Sixth Regiment, "The soldiers strolled about the Common, talking with their friends and acquaintances. Those who were so unfortunate as not to have any, soon succeeded in making both out of the crowd who were anxious to hear all the news that was to be heard."

August 23.

The Seventeenth Regiment, en route to the war, passed through the city and Common.

August.

The Pond in the Public Garden was prepared and completed.

September 4.

The Twentieth Regiment on their way to the war passed through Boston and the Common.

September 24.

Jerome Bonaparte had a public reception in Boston and visited the Common.

OCTOBER 8.

The Twenty-second Regiment, en route to the war, went through Boston and the Common.

NOVEMBER 11.

The Twenty-third Regiment, going South, passed through the city and drew many to the Common.

NOVEMBER 19.

The Ninth Connecticut Regiment went through Boston en route to Lowell. Many walked to the Common.

DECEMBER 19.

The First Cavalry arrived at Faneuil Hall, after the parade many went down to the Common.

Many regiments, en route to or returning home from the war, passed through Boston and encamped on the Common when boys would fill the soldiers canteens from the fountain, on the corner of Charles and Beacon Streets, taking six and eight at a time.

The famous Ellsworth Zouaves gave their marvelous "lightning drill," before many spectators, on the Common one afternoon.

Two large soldiers, belonging to a Maine Regiment, gave a bear-dance greatly amusing a number of people, on the Common.

Recruit tents stood in different places—one on the big hill on the Common—when speeches were made urging men to enlist. One young fellow declared that he'd enlist if he were a "paralyzed corpse" calling forth loud cheers and great mirth.

The "Headquarters of the Recruiting Committee, Flagstaff Hill, Boston Common," was lithographed and published by J. H. Bufford, Boston, September, 22, 1862. It is in the Boston Public Library.

Five granite basins, with fountains, were placed in different parts of the Public Garden which was also beautified by ornamental work. One basin, contains a beautiful marble statue presented by John D. Bates. A beautiful figure was also presented by Mrs. Tudor.

Mechanics, firemen, etc., occasionally met to play ball on the Common.

1862 JANUARY 2.

The Twelfth Regiment, going South through Boston, drew many to the Common.

JANUARY 3.

General Benjamin F. Butler reviewed his New England Regiment in Boston where great crowds gathered on the streets and Common.

JANUARY 11.

The Twenty-eighth Regiment, en route to the war, passed through Boston. Many walked on the Common.

JANUARY 25.

The Eighth New Hampshire Regiment coming home, via Boston, caused a number to go to the Common.

February 15.

The Fourteenth Regiment going to war, via Boston, caused an unusual number to go to the Common.

February 18.

The Thirteenth Regiment going South, through Boston, drew many to the Common.

April 11.

Shiloh and other recent Union victories were celebrated by the firing of a salute of one hundred guns on the Common.

May 12.

Governor Brownlow was given a public reception in Boston and went to the Common.

June 7.

The West Street gate at the Common was completed.

July 28.

Patrick Rafferty, a member of the Thirty-third Regiment, while addressing a crowd on the Common, was contradicted by a man whom the by-standers seized and threw into the Frog Pond.

August 14.

The departure, through Boston, of the Thirty-third Regiment, for the South, drew a large number to the Common.

August 19.

The Sixteenth Regiment went through Boston causing many to go to the Common.

August 21.

The departure of the Seventeenth Regiment through Boston—for the war, made the Common more crowded than usual.

August 22.

The Thirty-fifth Regiment passed through Boston for the war. Crowds on the Common.

August 26.

The Thirty-eighth Regiment passed through Boston for the war causing a crowd on the Common.

August 27.

The departure of the Nineteenth Regiment, via Boston, caused great crowds on the Common.

August 27.

A Great War Meeting was held on the Common, stands were erected, in different places, where eloquent speeches were made by Governor Andrew, Edward Everett, Robert C. Winthrop and others. The *Advertiser,* says: "On no occasion which the war has given rise to has the expression of the people been so general and so marked by patriotic fervor as in the grand celebration of yesterday. Business was universally suspended by common consent, and the suggestion for a procession and mass meeting in aid of the city recruitment met with a hearty response.....The affair was essentially popular; men in citizen's dress and distinguished only by the badges of their respective callings, and the colors and mottoes which symbolize the common cause, united in the long procession, and listened to the eloquent appeals from the various stands on the Common......Early in the afternoon the various associations proposing to join in the procession began to assemble on the Common near Park Street.... The various civic and military organizations entered the Common by the West Street gate and were at once conducted into line by the Marshals. The procession was formed and paraded through the city in accordance with the well arranged programme.

AUGUST 29.

The departure of the Third Regiment drew many to the Common.

AUGUST 29.

General Corcoran had a reception in Boston visiting the Common.

AUGUST 29.

The Forty-fourth (Boston) Regiment went to the war when many assembled on the Common.

SEPTEMBER 2.

The Twentieth Regiment, going South, passed through the city. Some went to the Common.

SEPTEMBER 5.

The Thirty-ninth Regiment, going away, drew a number to the Common while passing through the city.

SEPTEMBER 8.

The Fortieth Regiment left for the war, via Boston, drew a number to the Common.

SEPTEMBER 9.

Funeral honors for the death of General Fletcher Webster drew many on the streets and Common.

SEPTEMBER 9.

A Special was appointed for the Public Garden.

OCTOBER 18.

The Twenty-third Regiment left for the war, via Boston, crossing the Common.

OCTOBER 20.

The Twenty-seventh Regiment went South, via Boston, when an unusually large number waved handkerchiefs on the streets and Common.

OCTOBER 21.

The Twenty-first Regiment passed through Boston, and crossed the Common, en route for the war.

OCTOBER 22.

The Twenty-second Regiment went to the war, via Boston. Many went to the Common.

OCTOBER 26.

The Twenty-eighth Regiment passed through the city, and Common, en route to the war.

NOVEMBER 5.

The Forty-first, Forty-third and Forty-fifth Regiments passed through Boston to the war causing a greater number than usual on the Common.

NOVEMBER 9.

The Forty-sixth and Forty-seventh Regiments passed through Boston for the war. A large number assembled on the Common.

NOVEMBER 19.

The Fiftieth Regiment going to the war, via Boston, drew many to the Common.

NOVEMBER 25.

The Fifty-first Regiment went through Boston, and the Common, en route to the war.

Anthony Trollope, in North America,—in alluding to Boston, says: "There is an Athenaeum, and a State Hall, and a fashionable street,—Beacon Street, very like Piccadilly as it runs along the Green Park,—and there is the Green Park opposite to the Piccadilly, called Boston Common. Beacon Street and Boston Common are very pleasant......I became enamored of Boston at last. Beacon Street was very pleasant to me, and the view over Boston Common was dear to my eyes. Even the State House, with its great yellow painted dome, became sightly; and the sunset over the western waters that encompass the city beats all other sunsets that I have seen."

A new iron fence was put around the Public Garden replacing the old wooden one.

1863 JANUARY 13.

General Benjamin F. Butler was tendered a grand reception at Faneuil Hall. He often went to the Common.

JANUARY 14.

A California Cavalry Company had a reception in Boston and visited the Common.

JANUARY 29.

General George B. McClellan had a reception at Faneuil Hall and went to the Common.

MAY 3.

The departure of the Fifty-fourth (colored) Regiment from Boston caused much enthusiasm on the streets and Common.

MAY 12.

Ralph Waldo Emerson and Walt Whitman walked up and down the Mall—on the Common—"vigorously discussing" the desirability of publishing Whitman's "Children of Adam." Notwithstanding the objections of "Concord's Bard," Whitman followed another of his precepts—"Insist on Yourself" as expressed in the essay on Self Reliance.

WEDNESDAY, JUNE 10.

An enthusiastic welcome was given to the Forty-fourth Regiment on their return from the war, when a large crowd gathered on the Common and filling the Charles Street Mall. The *Advertiser* says, on the following day: "The guns were then stacked and the men broke ranks. At this moment the ladies could restrain their feelings no longer. Propriety gave way to nature, and they rushed with open arms upon lovers, brothers, husbands, sons,—and perhaps cousins,—a female avalanche of streaming riband and fluttering silks. The brave fellows stood the shock like men.

They deployed as skirmishers and attempted to foil the attacking party with their own weapons; but were presently captured and led, willing prisoners, to the refreshment tables, where a tempting array of flowers and edibles was presented. The male relatives, presumably came in for their share of the greeting. After an hour or so spent in social conversation, affectionate questions and affectionate answers, the men were again brought into line and went through with a dress-parade, to the great satisfaction of the spectators. The regiment was then dismissed and the men will have a furlough till Monday, when they will probably go to Readville and be mustered out to the service."

June 26.

The return of the Fifth Regiment, from the war, caused many to assemble on the Common.

July 2.

The Twenty-third Maine Regiment, returning home, reached Boston when many went to the Common.

July 14.

The draft caused a great riot in Boston and much excitement on the Common.

The Draft Riot started in the slums on the North End where officers, while serving papers, in Prince Street, were cruelly beaten by the mob, who, having conquered a small number of police, were now reinforced by large numbers coming out of the tenements and saloons of Endicott, Charlestown, and other neighboring streets. An attempt was made to seize the cannon in the gun house on Cooper Street which was defended by a few regulars from Fort Warren. Several soldiers were killed and wounded and the doors nearly demolished when a general discharge into the mob caused them to scatter and retreat to Dock Square. Eight rioters were killed. Some stragglers went to the Common.

AUGUST 23.

The return of the Forty-eighth Regiment drew many to the Common

---

OCTOBER 1.

A park was laid out on the Common.

OCTOBER 22.

General Meagher visited Boston and the Common.

The Fifty-fourth (colored) Regiment reviewed by Governor Andrew when Frederick Douglas, whose two sons were in the ranks, was seated on the platform, stood, facing the capitol of the State, upon the corner of the Common, on their departure for Fort Wagner where their ranks were depleted and their Colonel (Shaw) was killed. When the attack was over the enemy, asked to deliver the body of the Colonel, replied "We've buried him with his niggers."

The historic Hancock mansion was demolished.

1864 JANUARY 17.

The Twenty-fifth Regiment returned home going to the Common.

JANUARY 22.

General Burnside was given a public reception in Boston visiting the Common.

FEBRUARY 8.

The Nineteenth Regiment returned from the war.

FEBRUARY 26, 27.

The return of the Twenty-fourth, Eighteenth and the New Hampshire Regiments drew many to the Common.

MARCH 19.

The return of the Thirtieth Regiment drew a greater crowd than usual to the Common.

APRIL 2.

The arrival of the Twenty-sixth Regiment.

APRIL 21.

The Thirty-first and Thirty-second Regiments came back.

MAY 22.

The Russian Embassy's fleet arrived in Boston harbor. Many officers and men visited the Common.

MAY 23.

Peacocks were put in the Deer Park on the Common.

MAY 28.

The First Regiment came home and went to Faneuil Hall and were mustered out on the Common.

JUNE 8.

The Russian Men of War—the Vitiar and the Osliaba—anchored in the harbor when the sailors, coming ashore, visited the Common where they were welcomed by the boys of the Latin and High Schools with a reception and collation.

JUNE 11.

The Ninth Regiment arrived home.

JUNE 15.

The Second New Hampshire Regiment came home via Boston and the Common.

JUNE 20.

The Eleventh Regiment arrived from the South.

JULY 1.

The Twelfth Regiment returned from the war.

JULY 21.

The Thirteenth, Fifteenth and Sixteenth Regiments, all came back from the war filling the streets and Common.

JULY 23.

Funeral honors for Colonel John Chambers drew many to the streets and Common.

NOVEMBER 3.

The Forty-second Regiment—Colonel Burrell, having performed good service at New Orleans, Brashear City, Baton Rouge, Houston, Galveston, etc., returned via Washington where they were reviewed by President

Lincoln at the White House, and arriving in Boston, passed their last night at Faneuil Hall and, the next morning, were mustered out on the Common.

Squirrels disappeared from the Common during the winter.

1865 JANUARY 19.

Funeral services for the death of Hon. Edward Everett, drew many to the streets and Common.

WASHINGTON'S BIRTHDAY, FEB. 22.

When the news came that President Lincoln had signed the Emancipation Bill flags were displayed all over the city, bells rang, while the utmost excitement prevailed. One hundred guns were fired on the Common.

APRIL 10.

The surrender of Lee's army, at Appomattox, caused tremendous excitement and rejoicing. Flags hung from nearly every building, bells pealed forth, twenty steam engines were drawn screeching through the streets, while cannon roared on the Common.

APRIL 15.

News of the assassination of President Lincoln caused all public buildings to be draped in mourning. Many sad faces were seen on the Common.

JUNE 1.

Funeral honors for the death of President Lincoln drew great crowds to the streets and Common.

JUNE 12.

Shortly prior to the unveiling of the Hamilton Statue, on Commonwealth Avenue, Mayor Lincoln wrote that no better locality could have been selected as it had been proposed to place Ball's Equestrian Statue of Washington on the Common or Public Garden.

JULY 4.

The statue of Horace Mann was inaugurated in the State House grounds when addresses were made by Governor Andrew, John D. Philbrick, President Hill, Dr. S. G. Howe, and others. A large number of eminent men and women sat on the platform in the rear, the green was filled with school children while crowds stood around and walked on the Common.

JULY 19.

General George G. Meade visited Boston and the Common.

JULY 31.

Lieutenant-General U. S. Grant made his first visit to Boston and the Common.

MONDAY, SEPTEMBER 18.

The dedication of the City Hall was intended to be held on the anniversary of the Foundation of Boston, but, which occurring on Sunday, the exercises were held the next day, at noon. The address was delivered by Mayor Frederick W. Lincoln, Jr. Some walked down to the Common.

DECEMBER 15.

On the return of the Fifty-fifth (colored) Regiment they were welcomed by a great procession. Many went to the Common.

DECEMBER 22.

The battle flags of the Massachusetts Regiments were deposited to the charge of the Commonwealth, on the Park Street Mall.

Many regiments returned, with thinned ranks and tattered flags, from the war, and, war bronzed veterans, mustered out, walked, talking with friends, on the Common.

The bill authorizing the rebuilding of the Beacon Hill Monument (with the old tablets which were preserved) by the Bunker Hill Monument Association was passed by the Legislature.

Dr. Holmes, in the Autocrat, alludes to the Public Garden as "my Garden."

Longfellow's poem "To the River Charles," contains the verse:

"While yon shadowy woodlands hide thee,
And thy waters disappear,
Friends I love have dwelt beside thee
And have made thy margin dear."

1866 JULY 13.

General William T. Sherman visited Boston and the Common.

October 12.

Schoolboys, in their bright uniforms, made a pleasant sight drilling on the Common.

November 14.

Astronomers predicted a shower of meteors which were to be heralded by ten strokes of the bells and the watchmen's rattles. A large crowd came to the Common, but the meteors did not appear.

December 6.

The Liberty Pole was removed to the little hill on the Common.

1867 May 15.

A baseball game was played between the *Lowell's* and the Harvard boys on the Common. Won by the *Lowell's* in a score of 37 to 28.

June 1.

The baseball grounds, on the Common, were divided by ropes and stakes watched by policemen.

June 1.

The stone bridge, across the Pond, in the Public Garden was completed.

June 17.

The Athletics, of Philadelphia, defeated the *Eon's,* of Portland, in a game of baseball played on the Common. Score 88 to 22.

July 4.

A Liberty Pole was raised in the Public Garden.

OCTOBER 1.

A sanitary station house was placed on a little hill on the Common.

OCTOBER 7.

General Philip H. Sheridan visited Boston and the Common.

NOVEMBER 18.

A bronze statue of Hon. Edward Everett Story, the sculptor, was made in Munich and presented to the city. It stands on the northerly side of the Public Garden.

DECEMBER.

The State House was remodelled and repaired.

Prospectus on a map: "Town of Boston in New England," in 1722, "Aetatus Luce 60" by Capt. John Bonner, "Engraved from a copy in the possession of William Taylor, Esq., and published by George G. Smith. Engraved 1867, 91 Washington, opposite State Street, Boston," and also stamped "1835—Scale of 1/2 a Mile."

"Explanation—Boston N. E."

A. Planted An Dom 1630	Streets 42, Lanes 36, Alleys 22; Houses near 3000, 1000 Brick, Rest Timber, near 12,000 people.
B. Old North, 1650	
C. Old South, 1660	
D. Ana Baptist, 1680	Great Fires.
E. Chh. of England, 1688	First, 1653
F. Brattle St. Church, 1699	Second, 1659
G. Quakers, 1710	Third, 1679

H.	New North, 1714	Fourth, 1683
I.	New South, 1716	Fifth, 1690
K.	French, 1716	Sixth, 1691
L.	New No. Brick, 1721	Seventh, 1702
a.	Town House	Eighth, 1711
b.	Governor's House	Gen. Small-pox
c.	South Grammar School	First, 1640
d.	North Grammar School	Second, 1660
e.	Writing School	Third, 1677-1678 Fourth, 1680-1690
f.	Writing School	Fifth, 1702
g.	Almshouse	Sixth, 1721."
h.	Bridewell	

The map also designates many points including the "Harbour," "Common," "Mill Pond," "Charles River," "Ferry to Chelsea," etc., and also a fac-simile in writing, viz.: "I have examined this plan and found it to be an exact copy of the original. (Signed) Stephen P. Fuller, Surveyor, Boston, July 2, 1835."

1868 MARCH 20.

Kit Carson and the Ute Indians visited Boston and the Common.

MAY 27.

The Military companies had a champion drill on the Common.

JUNE 3.

The Brewer Fountain first threw forth its bright and sparkling stream. An exquisite bronze modelled after the design of Liénard of Paris, with figures representing Neptune and Amphrite, Acis and Galatea. It was made in Paris and was presented by Mr. Gardner

Brewer—a most public spirited citizen, to Boston. It is not only a feature of the Common, but has been copied by the cities of Lyons and Bordeaux and the late Viceroy of Egypt.

JUNE 26.

The corner of Tremont and Boylston Streets, on the Common, was cut off for one night.

JUNE 27.

Near the north westerly corner is the monument presented by Thomas Lee, Esq. The presentation address was delivered by Dr. Henry J. Bigelow when it was formally accepted by the Mayor.

JUNE.

The Mayor authorized that a corner of the Common, on the south side of Boylston street, should be cut off and rounded.

JULY 8.

The Twenty-second New York Regiment—Captain Vose—visited Boston and the Common.

AUGUST 20.

The Chinese Embassy, crossing the Pacific to San Francisco journeyed across the Continent and reached Boston at nine a. m. with Hon. Anson Burlingame, envoy extraordinary and minister plenipotentiary, accompanied by Chih-Ta-jin and Sun Ta-jin to partake of the hospitalities offered by the city. Entering their carriages, at the Western Avenue crossing, they were escorted through the city in the following order:

The Chief Marshall.

Aids: Police Captains R. H. Wilkins and S. G. Adams, Mounted Police officers under the command of Paul J. Vinal.

Cavalry Band.

Mayor Lucius Slade and Staff.

Company B First Battalion Light Dragoons, Capt. Barney Hull. His Honor the Mayor and Hon. Anson Burlingame in a barouche drawn by four horses. The Chairman of the Committee, Chief Ta-jin and Mr. Brown, First Secretary—in a barouche drawn by four horses. Alderman Benjamin James, Sun Ta-jin and Mr. De Champs (Second Secretary) in a barouche. The President of the Common Council, Councilman Pickering, Fung Lao-Yeh and Tah Lao-Yeh, interpreters, in a barouche. Councilmen Denny and Snow, Teh Lao-Yeh and Keuay Lao-Yeh, interpreters, in a barouche. Followed by carriages containing Ting Lao-Yeh, Lien Lao-Yeh; also, Kang Lao-Yeh, Chooang Lao-Yeh, the Scribes and Tsi; the physician to the Embassy. Carriages containing reporters for the daily papers and the servants of the Embassy, Company C, First Battalion of Light Dragoons, Captain George Curtis.

The route of the procession was as follows: Through Western Avenue, Center, Marcella and Highland Streets, Eliot Square, Dudley, Warren and Washington Streets, Chester Square, Tremont and Worcester Streets, Harrison Avenue, Newton and Washington Streets, Union Square, Tremont, Boylston and Arlington Streets, Commonwealth Avenue, Berkeley, Beacon, Park, Tremont, Winter, Summer, Devonshire and Franklin Streets, counter-marching around the flag staff, through Devonshire, Milk, India, State, Washington, and School Streets to the Parker House where the guests alighted.

Salutes in honor of a Foreign Minister, were fired from Washington Square at the Highlands and from the Common.

AUGUST 21, NOON.

A public reception was given by the Embassy at Faneuil Hall.

A banquet was also given at St. James Hotel, Mayor Shurtleff, presiding, who, after an address of welcome and music by Gilmore's Band, announced the toasts, in the following order, and their respondents:

First: "The President of the United States." The band performed the American National Air.

Second: "The Emperor of China." The band then performed the Chinese National Air.

Third: "The Chinese Embassy," Mr. Burlingame.

Fourth: "The Commonwealth of Massachusetts." Governor Bullock.

Fifth: "The Supplementary Treaty with China." Hon. Charles Sumner.

Sixth: "Diplomacy." Hon. Caleb Cushing. Cheers were given for the only minister to China who bore a Chinese name—"Coo-Shing."

Seventh: "The Union of the Farthest East and the Farthest West." Ralph Waldo Emerson.

Eighth: "The Commercial Relations between China and the United States." Charles A. Nazro, Esq.

Ninth: "The Press." Mr. Edwin P. Whipple.

SEPTEMBER 2.

Last day of the visit of the Embassy to Boston, they had visited the City Hall, the Institute of Technology, the Public Library, the City Hospital, the Waltham Watch Company and the Bunker Hill Monument.

Their Oriental dress attracted many persons as they walked through the Common.

NOVEMBER 20.

An interesting incident, on the Common, was the placing of a bear in the enclosure with the deer causing a stampede of deer.

NOVEMBER.

Meteoric showers, predicted, fell beautifully on the Common.

A stone was laid out from West Street to Park Square, on the Common.

1869 SPRING.

The Common, which had more than once been the scene of a base ball match between the Harvard's and the Lowell's was plowed over and games ceased. The Lowell now had won many victories. In six years it had played ninety-nine games and won seventy. Baseball had now become a factor in local politics as the loss of the Common for a practice ground led to the formation of a baseball element that subsequently helped to elect a mayor and alderman for the restoration of the right.

MAY 26.

Firing by electricity was witnessed on the Common.

MAY.

The Mutual's of New York played the Tri-mountains whom they defeated in a score of 69 to 17. They also played the Harvard's defeating them by 43 to 11, and finally the Lowell's who made 21 runs against the Mutual's 26. These games were played on the Common.

June 10.

The world renowned Red Stockings, of Cincinnati, visited Boston. This celebrated nine, which has never been equalled, was composed of George Wright, short stop; Harry Wright, centre field; Douglas Allison, catcher; Fred Waterman, third base; Charlie Gould, first base; Andy Leonard, left field; Calvin McVey, right field; Charlie Sweasey, second base; and Asa Brainard, pitcher. They played with the Lowell's, on the Common, making a score of 29 runs against 9.

June 11.

They played the Tri-mountains scoring 40 runs to 12.

June 12.

They beat the Harvard's in a score of 30 to 11. These games were witnessed, amid great cheering, by thousands of spectators who were seated on the stands, erected on the Parade Ground, on the Common.

June 16.

General Butler's Brigade was reviewed by President Grant on Tremont Street, South End and the Common.

July 3.

The equestrian bronze statue of Washington, modelled by Ball and cast at the Chicopee Works, was placed in the Public Garden. The dedicatory address was made by Hon. Alexander H. Rice.

The equestrian statue of Washington was unveiled in the Public Garden.

SEPTEMBER 8.

A terrible wind storm blew down the Coliseum and several other buildings and did much damage in the city. One of the large remaining limbs of the "Old Elm" fell and a number of trees were uprooted on the Common.

OCTOBER 10, 5.30 A. M.

A slight shock of earthquake was felt on the Common.

DECEMBER 11.

Baseball players became an element in politics and determined to elect a Mayor and Alderman in their interests. The baseball ballot was designated by a large red ball. Whatever may have resulted the following Spring, Mayor Shurtleff granted to the boys the lower end of the Common as a playground.

Boys sleds, on the Common, had many fanciful names, viz.: "Comet," "Cave Adsum," "Dancing Feather," "Lullah," "Long Coast," etc.

The house-sparrow was introduced, by the city government, to the Common and the Public Garden.

1870 MAY 25.

A magnificent military display on the Common.

JUNE 25.

The School Regiment, witnessed by many spectators, drilled on the Common.

OCTOBER 20, AT 11 A. M.

A slight shock of earthquake was felt on the Common.

CLOSE OF THE SEVENTIES.

Coasting was always a favorite pastime on the Common. The "Long Coast" ran from the corner of Park and Beacon Streets to the West Street Gate, and for some distance along the Mall. Another coast ran from Joy toward Boylston Street. Both were sprinkled at night to make the ice smooth on the following day. Bridges covered the coasts where many persons watched the boys up to eleven o'clock at night. Much rivalry existed in their speed with many amusing upsets. Coasting on the Common led to several serious accidents, and, discountenanced during the *seventies*, the bridges were taken away and gravel scattered over the hills.

In winter the snowball fight between the West Enders and the South Enders created scenes of great merriment on the Common when the West Enders would strive to drive their antagonists to Boylston Street.

Owing to various changes on the Common the Public Garden had now become a favorite children's resort with sand boxes and swings.

1871 MAY 31.

Training day on the Common.

JUNE 5.

The Kansas, with Little Raven, were in Boston and went to the Common.

SUNDAY, JUNE 18.

Colonel James Fisk's Ninth New York Regiment, on a visit to Boston, held religious services on the Common.

JUNE.

Flagstaff removed from big to little hill.

JULY 20.

A slight shock of earthquake was felt on the Common.

SEPTEMBER 18, AT 12.55.

The cornerstone of the Soldiers' Monument was laid on the Common.

DECEMBER 8.

The Grand Duke Alexis had a reception at the Boston Theatre and visited the Common.

1872 JUNE 17.

The World's Musical Festival commenced which, lasting for twenty days, was attended by from 30,000 to 70,000 and even 100,000 persons each day, and causing many people to throng the streets. Great crowds visited the Common.

SATURDAY, NOVEMBER 9.

Soon after seven o'clock p. m.

A fire broke out in the business portion of the city—corner of Summit and Kingston Streets. The flames gaining great headway before the alarm was sounded, while the horses, all suffering from epizootic, were incapacitated for duty. Extra men, who had been appointed, drew the engines to the fire. The flames, witnessed by thousands of spectators, spread down Summer Street, along the lower side of Washington, as far as the Old South Church and crossed Milk Street, thence eastward and northward, to the water front and beyond Pearl Street. An extra police force and a brigade of militia restored a kind of order out of the excitement, while trucks drawn by clerks, conveyed merchandise to the different depots, merchants carried valuable papers to remote places of safety and poor people, south of Summer Street, all through the night, dragged their household effects to the Common. The flames lit the sky for a distance of sixty miles.

In the great fire that laid waste to so large a portion of Boston it was thought providential that the old landmarks were preserved, viz., Christ Church, Faneuil Hall, the Old State House, the Old South Church, Kings Chapel and the Park Street Spire, besides which the Common might have lost its gates and the "Old Elm."

1873 JUNE 13.

A flower show was exhibited in a tent on the Common.

JUNE 23.

Annual drill of the school children on the Common.

OCTOBER 2.

A military company from Providence drilled on the Common.

An effort was made to lay another horse car track on Tremont Street when the fence on the Common was taken down, but replaced in a year.

The famous Paddock elms planted on the edge of the Common by Mayor Adino Paddock, the first coachmaker of the town, whose house stood opposite the burying ground—were removed to make way for traction improvements. It caused great regret.

It is said of the Common that its beauty is surpassed by its historic association.

The Charles River; says the American Cyclopedia—"A stream rising in Worcester County, Massachusetts, and flowing through Norfolk and Middlesex Counties into Boston harbor. The towns on its banks are Hopkinton, Milford, Bellingham, Franklin, Medway, Medfield, Sherburne, Dover, Dedham, Needham, Natick, Newton, Waltham, Watertown, Brighton and Cambridge. It affords numerous sites for mills and factories, and is navigable to Watertown, 7 m. west of Boston. The lower part of the course is the favorite training place for the boat clubs of Harvard University. It is now proposed to draw from the upper part of this river an additional supply of water for Boston."

1875 JANUARY 27.

Large, elaborate, sleighs came into use on the Common, the *Globe* says: "It is a long, double, runner of the usual pattern, painted red, with a head light like a juvenile locomotive, and a steering apparatus on the tiller principle. It is cushioned quite elegantly and has side rests for the feet of the coasters, of whom it will accommodate eight or ten. A large, white, streamer ornaments the prow, and there are brass trimmings and handles along the sides." It cost two hundred and forty dollars.

JANUARY.

King Kalakuana, of the Sandwich Islands, visits Boston and the Common.

FEBRUARY 13.

Harper's Weekly (New York), contains a picture of "Coasting on Boston Common," drawn by C. S. Reinhart from a sketch by E. H. Garrett.

JUNE 17.

The Centennial Anniversary of the battle of Bunker Hill was celebrated by a grand civic and military procession when the streets were thronged with strangers from all parts of the country. Public buildings, private dwellings, and places of business along the route of the procession, and in fact everywhere, were handsomely decorated with flags, bunting and flowers, while inscriptions denoted battlefield localities and various deeds of valor. At ten o'clock a. m. the troops started from the Common and passing out at the corner of Charles Street and Boylston Street marched through Boylston, Tremont and Beacon Streets passing the reviewing stand in front of the State House.

The History of the (New York) Seventh Regiment (1890) by Colonel Emmons Clark, in a description of the visit of the "Seventh" to Boston, says: "At eight a. m. the Regiment assembled at Horticultural Hall, and was escorted by the Eighth Massachusetts Regiment to its place in line near the Common......The streets leading to the State House were thronged with people and almost impassable and at every point the Regiment was received with great enthusiasm. In front of the State House a large platform had been erected, and the troops passed in review before Governor Gaston, who was attended by Generals Sherman, Burnside, and Pope, Vice President Wilson, the Governors of several States, the mayors of the principal cities of the country, and many other distinguished officials, civic and military. As the Seventh Regiment approached the reviewing stand and debouched from the narrow street into the State House Plaza, the column of platoons was formed into column of companies and the promptness and accuracy with which the maneouvre was performed excited the astonishment and admiration of the immense throng of distinguished people assembled in the vicinity."

1876 FEBRUARY 16.

The "Old Elm," breaking at the base, fell to the ground. It had long had a large decayed cavity, near the ground, where boys hid playing hide and seek. People rushed to the Common to obtain pieces of wood for keepsakes. A chair was made which is now in the Public Library, and veneered pictures, by the city; one is in the library of the Historical Society.

MAY.

A stone curb was laid next to Tremont Street on the Common.

JULY 4.

The Centennial celebration: Multitudes walked on the Common—passing many temporary booths erected on the Malls—during the day, while between 50,000 and 100,000 persons gathered to see a grand display of fireworks at night, but who were much disappointed as a high wind greatly marred the effects.

1877 JANUARY 28.

The meetings of Moody and Sankey begun at the Tabernacle, on Tremont Street, and, lasting for thirteen weeks, caused many to walk to the Common at the close of the afternoon services.

SEPTEMBER 17.

The Army and Navy Monument on Flagstaff Hill was dedicated with appropriate ceremonies at which President Hayes and staff were present and a vast concourse of military societies, clubs, organizations and citizens. The inscription—written by President Charles William Eliot, of Harvard University, reads: "To the men of Boston who died for their country on Land and Sea, in the War which kept the Union whole, destroyed Slavery, and maintained the Constitution, the Grateful City has built this Monument, that their Example may speak to Coming Generations." The Monument is of Maine granite, 70 feet high and solid masonry foundation. Three steps lead to a square stone platform with a plinth above, nine feet high, where at the corners are pedestals with bronze statues, representing, America, Peace, the Sailor, History, the Soldier. And *mezzo relievos,* viz.: Scenes of Departure for the War, the Sanitary Commission, Return from the War, the Navy.

The Monument cost $75,000.

In the evening the Monument and Fountain were illuminated by calcium lights; two opposite lights on the shores of the Pond focused and illuminated the Fountain in successive colors—while, red, blue, green, yellow, and purple. The Boston Cadet Band, under the leadership of John C. Mullaly, rendered the following selections during the evening.

(1) March, "Helmstadt," first time........*Plaade*
(2) Overture, "Crown Diamonds"..........*Auber*
(3) Concert Waltz, "Norman"...........*Strauss*
(4) Cornet Solo, "Brilliant"..............*Arban*

Performed by Walter Emerson.

(5) Grand Selection, "Dinorah".......*Meyerbeer*
(6) Caprice, "La Baladine".............*Lysberg*
(7) Potpourri, "Girofle Girofla"..........*Lecocq*
(8) Fantaisie for Piccolo ....*De Carlo*

Performed by A. Damm.

(9) Potpourri, "Harvard" ....*Mullaly*
(10) Galop, "Fairy Queen".........*Sydney Smith*
(11) Medley of National and Popular Airs.

The "Department for the War" depicted on the bronze *bas-relief*—tablet—Martin Millmore—on the Army and Navy Monument, on the Common, shows Governor Andrew, standing on the State House steps, near by are Longfellow, Archbishop Williams, Rev. Dr. A. H. Vinton and other notabilities while General Butler, Colonel Shaw and Colonel Cass appear in uniform.

Five Grand Malls,—the Beacon Street, the Park Street, the Tremont Street, the Boylston Street, and the Charles Street, with their travelling amusements: Punch and Judy, Cameros, Telescopes, Scales, Blowing Machines, attract visitors to the Common.

The Massachusetts Charitable Association desiring to erect a temporary exhibition building on the Common, were met by a strong remonstrance by the citizens who defeated the project.

Wind mill, Powder House, Flag Staff and Monument Hills on the Common.

The *Dial says of the Old South Clock*: "For years the Old South Clock has been a Boston institution; passersby, whether for business, or pleasure, or travel, have made it a point, no matter how fast they were walking, to look up and see what time it is, and to regulate watches and their arrangements accordingly. And when there was a rumor, or worse, that the Old South was to be destroyed, the most indifferent and heartless regretted the loss of their old monitor as a threat to cut out a piece from their daily life......

The Old South Dial still stands—and goes too,—and it is intended and resolved that it shall stand and go for the information and correction of Washington Street and its passers for many years to come...... The key of our daily chimes is, *The Old South shall be saved*......

The True Value of the Old South.

The Old Church stands today a fit emblem of the State the Puritans founded, and the hierarchy they established. The dramatic events recur to the memory in rapid succession; the banishment of Williams; the trial of Mrs. Hutchinson; the contest with the restored Stuarts; the failure of the Puritan theory of government; the deadly fanaticism of the witchcraft delusion, and then the lethargy of the provincial times in the days when England's prime minister boasted that she had no history, and our colonial assembly wrangled in true English fashion, with their governors over salaries and taxes. Close on these scenes followed the French war, concluding with the death of Wolfe and the downfall of the French power, paving the way for independence. In all the succeeding struggles with England resulting finally in the arbitration of the sword, the Old South itself shared, and the memories of those days are inseparable from the dumb materials of which it is composed."

Had the Old South Church been demolished every brick would have been kept as a keepsake and its wood taken away in pieces like the "Old Elm" on the Common.

The Common and the Old South Church are the historic land marks of Boston.

1878 JANUARY 19.

Great gathering of working men on the Common.

APRIL 28.

Party of Brigade Generals visited Boston and the Common.

JULY 4.

A flying machine was exhibited on the Common.

JULY 4.

Fireworks on the Common spoiled by the rain.

JULY 28.

Dennis Kearney, the Sand Lot orator from San Francisco, arrived in Boston and visited the Common.

SEPTEMBER 24.

Hon. James G. Blaine gave a political lecture at Faneuil Hall and went to the Common.

DECEMBER 22.

A statue of Sumner was placed in the Public Garden.

1879 MAY 16.

A walking match took place, under a big tent, on the Back Bay. Many walked over the Common.

MAY 22.

Parade and Review on the Common.

AUGUST 6.

The Poncas visited Boston and the Common.

OCTOBER.

The iron fence, on the east side of the Common, was removed to Mount Hope.

When Dean Stanley visited Boston his first wish, expressed to Edward Everett Hale, was that he might see the "Old Elm" on the Common.

1880 SEPTEMBER 17.

At the celebration of the 250th Anniversary of the settlement of Boston, the Winthrop Statue was unveiled with a reception at Faneuil Hall and exercises at the Old South Church. More than 230,000 people came from out of town to witness the immense procession which, owing to the throng, could hardly pass through Hanover Street.

The evening procession, with its torchlights and *tableaux,* was a notable feature. Gilmore's Band gave an evening concert on the Common when the following selections were performed:

Overture, "Semiramide" .... *Rossini*
Aria for Cornet, "The Lost Chord"......... *Sullivan*
Mr. J. Salcedo.
Grand Selection, "Gems of Opera"........ *Meyerbeer*
Trombone Solo, "Air and Variations"...... *Hartman*
Mr. F. Innes.
Finals, "William Tell" Overture............ *Rossini*
Euphronium Solo, "Concerts"............. *Raffayolo*
Sig. Raffayolo.
Galop: Characteristic, "Coney Island Races".... *Bosio*
Turkish March, "Advance and Retreat".... *Michaelis*
Piccolo Solo, variations on "Spring, Gentle Spring" *Riviere*
Sig. de Carlo.

New National Anthem, "Columbia"......... *Gilmore*

The concert lasted from 7.30 to 9.30 p. m.

The extent of the Common is forty-eight acres.

Three rows of decayed trees were removed from the east side of the Common.

The Public Garden is described as "a garden of statues, shrubbery, plants and flowers."

1882 JULY 11.

Re-dedication of the Old State House; address by William H. Whitmore, Esq. Many strolled on the Common.

The reservoir on Beacon Hill was being removed.

1885 NEW YEAR'S DAY.

A large reception was given at Howard Ticknors' when among those said to have been present were Mrs. Louise Chandler Moulton, Dr. Holmes, Professor Horsford, Aldrich, the author of Baby Bell, accompanied by his charming wife. Dean Hodges, Mrs. Ole Bull, who had given a large party the previous night, the Whipples, Oscar Fay Adams, Professor Lane of Harvard University, Arlo Bates, Mrs. Kate Gannett Wells, Mrs. Julia Ward Howe, Mrs. Maude Howe Elliott, Mrs. Harriet Prescott Spofford, authoress of "Amber Gods" and "A Thief in the Night," Mrs. Julius Eichberg and daughter, Mrs. Anna Eichburg King (now Mrs. John Lane of London). All were familiar with the Common.

APRIL 23.

Phillip Brooks, D. D., delivered the oration at the celebration of the 250th Anniversary of the Foundation of the Boston Latin School, saying that "at a much earlier period School Street and the Common, and the Charles River were a world in themselves, and that the ever recurring life of the new generations, boyhood opening into manhood, makes a perpetual inspiration. It is the systole and disastole of the city's heart."

NOVEMBER 17.

At the Sixth Reunion of the "Old School Boys of Boston," held at the *Hotel Vendome,* Mr. Guild, said, "I once came up through West Street to the Mall, when a game, of football was about to begin on Boston Common. There was quite a large assemblage of boys from the Mason Street (Adams) School and the Franklin School......We played baseball and hockey right on the Mall, and Boston Common was the playground of the Boston School boys."

1887

The "Old Corner Bookstore" erected after the fire of 1711, and where Anne Hutchinson held *seances,* stands on the corner of Washington and School Streets. It is older than any Boston church, thirty years older than the original Faneuil Hall, and almost as old as the outer walls of the Old State House. It has always been a centre where Hawthorne, Sprague, Willis, Whipple, Willard, Parsons, Emerson, Longfellow, Agassiz, Sumner, Whittier, Holmes, Lowell, Motley and hundreds of other bright literary stars have purchased books which they read during a stroll on the Common.

1888 NOVEMBER 5.

A barred owl and a small hawk were seen in adjoining trees on the Common.

The Crispus Attucks Monument was erected commemorating the victims of the Boston Massacre. The design shows "Revolution breaking the chains of tyranny" with the names of the martyrs and the scene of bloodshed.

Howells, in April Hopes,—describes the walk of Alice and Dan on the Beacon Street Path in the Public Garden, thus: "The benches on either side were filled with nurse-maids in charge of baby carriages, and of young children who were digging in the sand with their little beach shovels, and playing their games back and forth across the walk unrebuked by the indulgent policemen. A number of them had enclosed a square in the middle of the path with four of the benches, which they made-believe was a fort. The lovers had to walk round it, and the children, chasing one another, dashed into them headlong, or, backing off from pursuit, bumped up against them. They did not seem to know it, but walked slowly on without noticing; they were not aware of an occasional benchful of rather shabby young fellows who stared hard at the stylish girl and well-dressed young man talking together in such intense low tones, with rapid interchange of radiant glances."

1889

Jonathan and his Continent,—by Max O'Rell and Jack Allyn, says, "Boston is quite an English city, handsomely and solidly built. It has a Public Garden in the centre, the effect of which at night is superb. It is the most scholarly city in the United States, one of the greatest centres of learning in the world......The English spoken in Boston is purer than any to be heard elsewhere in the North. The voices are less harsh and nasal, the language ceases to be 'vury, vury Amurracan.' If you think yourself in England as you walk along the streets, the illusion becomes complete when you hear the well bred people speak."

Decade 1880-1890.

Among those who attend the "Friday's" of Mrs. Louise Chandler Moulton were Mr. and Mrs. Edmund Gosse of London; Matthew Arnold; W. D. Howells; Colonel T. W. Higginson; Helen Hunt; Mary Wilkins (now Mrs. Freeman); Mrs. Clement Waters; the writer on art, Alice Freeman; President of Wellesley College, afterwards Mrs. George Herbert Palmer; and Governor and Mrs. Claflin, and at other assemblies were Bliss Carmen and Edgar Fawcett, of New York, Arthur Foote who had rendered some of Mrs. Moulton's lyrics in music; also B. J. Lang and daughter who had set some of her songs. There were also the artists I. U. Gangengigl, Winthrop Pierce, John Enneking; Miss Porter and Miss Clarke the editors of Poet-Lore; Caroline Ticknor the young authoress; and among the clergy of Boston were Rev. Dr. Charles Gordon Ames and Mrs. Ames; Rev. Dr. Edward Everett Hale; Bishop Phillips Brooks; Rev. Bernard Carpenter, a brother of the Lord Bishop of Ripon, with many other distinguished people, all of whom regarded the Common with heartfelt pride.

1891 JANUARY 27.

A Frenchman in America,—by Max O'Rell, says, "Spent the whole evening wandering about Boston, and visiting a few interesting places, Beacon Street, the Public Gardens, and Commonwealth Avenue are among the finest thoro'fares I know. What enormous wealth is contained in those miles of huge mansions! The more I see of Boston the more it strikes me as a great English city. It has a character of its own, as no other American city has excepting perhaps Washington or Philadelphia. The solidity of the buildings, the parks, the quietness of the women's dresses, the absence of the twang in most of the voices, all remind you of England."

JULY 4.

The oration was delivered by Josiah Quincy in Faneuil Hall on the one hundred and fifteenth Anniversary of American Independence. Mr. Quincy said that scarcely a trace remained of the Boston that listened to the first Fourth of July oration (1783). Even the ground and even the harbor where the ships rode, that those of a century ago would scarcely recognize them. Nothing was left but the Old South Church, and Kings Chapel, the Old State House, the Ancient Burial Grounds and the Common.

NOVEMBER 31, AT 6 P. M.

A Golden Eyed Duck was seen in the Pond, in the Public Garden. On being approached he flapped his wings and flew toward the river.

1892 JANUARY 21.

The opening of the new building of the Boston Chamber of Commerce exercises were held at the old chamber at nine o'clock a. m., and the dedicatory exercises took place in the new chamber at half-past ten a. m., with an oration by Henry M. Whitney, at the close of which many went to the Common.

NOVEMBER.

An Acadian, or Sawwhet, owl was seen perched in an elm on Beacon Street, near the corner of Charles Street. A boy climbed the tree and came quite close to the owl when it flew away.

1893 JANUARY 26.

As the body of Phillips Brooks was borne from Trinity Church fully 10,000 people filled the Square all eager to catch a glimpse of the flower covered casket. In the out-door service they repeated the Lord's Prayer and all sang a hymn the air being played by trumpets. Many then walked to the Common.

When the remains of John Howard Payne, brought to this country from Tripoli, were re-interred in Oak Hill Cemetery, Washington, (June 9, 1883) fully 10,000 persons sang "Home, Sweet Home."

1893 NOVEMBER 23.

At the Fourteenth Reunion of the "Old School Boys of Boston," held at Young's Hotel, Mr. Lane, in relating an incident of childhood, said,—"When I was about four years of age, I started out to explore the town. Evidently I went down Purchase Street, and somehow I turned up Summer Street and brought upon Boston Common. "Old Wilson," the Crier, was despatched in search of me. I became very hungry and was much in grief, when a gentleman supplied me with gingerbread."

The proposed subway excavation, under the Common, caused a loud protest by the citizens of Boston which was only assented to after long and patient effort.

1895 JULY.

A large Christian convention met that drew thousands of people to the city many visiting the Common.

AUGUST.

The Knights Templar met in convention visiting King's Chapel, the Granary Burying Ground, the Old South Church, the Old State House, Faneuil Hall, Bunker Hill Monument and the Common. Great crowds were drawn to the city.

The subway stations on Tremont Street caused the

demolition of many old trees changing the picturesque outlook of the Common.

1896 SEPTEMBER 21.

A kingfisher flew over the Granary Burying Ground.

1897 MAY 31.

The monument in honor of Colonel Robert Gould Shaw of the Fifty-fourth (colored) Regiment was unveiled on the Common, when imposing ceremonies were held in Music Hall.

ORDER OF EXERCISES.

Music Patriotic Airs Instrumental

Meeting called to order by the Chief Marshall, and Chairman of the Committee on Monument called to preside.

Prayer....Rev. Edward H. Hall, Chaplain of the Day.

Greeting to His Excellency the Governor, Roger Wolcott, and Transfer of the Monument to His Honor the Mayor of Boston, by the Chairman of the Committee. Address of His Excellency, Governor Wolcott, Presiding officer. Acceptance by His Honor, Mayor Quincy.

Chorus, "Our Heroes."

Oration, "Battle Hymn of the Republic."

Address: President Booker T. Washington of Tuskegee Institute.

Music, "America"*—Instrumental.

*All joined in singing the air.

The bronze *bas relief* of the colored Regiment by Augustus St. Gaudens is one of the most artistic designs in the world.

The "Shaw Memorial" by Augustus St. Gaudens, has

been drawn in water colors by Charles Herbert Woodbury.

1898 April 25.

A winter Wren was seen in the Granary Burying Ground. It remained two days.

A stone was erected over the grave of James Otis the patriot orator of the Revolution,—"whose tongue was a flame of fire." The inscription reads: "Here lies buried James Otis, orator and patriot of the Revolution, famous for his argument against writs of assistance. Born 1725. Died 1783. Massachusetts Sons of the Revolution, 1898."

A stone boulder to be erected over the grave of the Revolutionary patriot Samuel Adams, which bears the inscription, "Here lies buried, Samuel Adams, Signer of the Declaration of Independence, Governor of this Commonwealth, a leader of men and an ardent Patriot. Born 1722. Died 1803. Massachusetts Society, Sons of the Revolution, 1898."

Boston Neighbors,—a charming novel, by Anna Blake Poor, says in the following extracts, "She almost hoped that he would not; and yet, as she entered the Public Garden a little later than usual the next morning, what a bound her heart gave as she saw him, evidently waiting for her, he said at once,... 'Miss Parke, will you walk a little way on the Common with me? There are not so many people there, and I have something I wish very much to say to you.'.... Simple as Margaret was, it was impossible for her not to see that Mr. Smith 'meant something,' only he did not have at all the air that she had supposed natural to the occasion. He looked neither confident nor doubtful, but calm and a little sad. Perhaps it was not the great 'something' after all, but an inferior 'something else.' She walked along with him in silence, her own face perplexed and doubtful enough. But when they reached the long walk across the loneliest corner of the Common, almost deserted, at this season, he said without further preface....'I must let you know how much I love you!' ....'Margaret, tell me if you can love me ever so little?' ....'How can I help it, when you have been so good to me?'....'Oh!' she went on, all radiant now with beauty and happiness."

1899

Orators appear on the Common on Sundays, and seen from club windows and dwellings, preach to the masses.

America today,—by William Archer, says; Boston, —"One can only repeat the obvious truth that it is like an exceptionally dignified and stately English town. One instinctively looks around for a cathedral, and finds the State House in its stead......She ought certainly to treat herself to a worthy Emerson Monument on the Common, whither the boy Emerson used to drive his mother's cows; not of course, a Gothic pile like that which commemorates the genius of Scott, but a statue by the incomparable St. Gaudens, under a modest classic canopy."

Close of the 19th Century.

The landscape color of Boston was greatly changed during the 19th century, by the filling up of the Back Bay, an arm of the Charles River, dividing the Common from the hills of Brookline and extending southerly and easterly to the Neck that connects Boston and Roxbury.

Plans to widen Tremont Street and to make a straight line of street cars over the Common to connect with Columbus Avenue or to make an open trench with pedestrian bridges caused a loud public sentiment to cry "Save the Common."

1900 MAY 9.

Barn Swallows, the earliest of the season, were seen in the Public Garden. They generally come in the latter part of May.

MAY 15.

A Gray-Cheeked Thrush was first seen in the Public Garden.

MAY 19.

A Golden Winged Warbler was seen in the Public Garden.

MAY 20.

A Prothonotary Warbler, in bright orange yellow plumage was seen flying through the air side of the Pond, in the Public Garden.

MAY 20.

A Black Warbler was seen, on the grass, in the Public Garden.

MAY 20.

Two Yellow Breasted Chats were seen in the grass, near the Washington Equestrian Statue, in the Public Garden.

MAY 23.

A Prairie Warbler came into the Public Garden. They are rarely seen.

MAY 23.

A Scarlet Tanager, with bright plumage, flew among the boughs of the trees around the Pond, on the Island, in the Public Garden.

MAY 24.

The last visit of two Wood Pewees in the Public Garden. One was in song the other silent.

DECEMBER 31.

The Dawn of the New Century

was observed by appropriate exercises:

At a quarter of an hour before midnight the State House was lighted by a vast array of swinging lanterns with a vast concourse of people over and on the Common. The Handel, Haydn and Cecilia Societies, four cornetists, Governor Crane, Dr. Hale, and several other persons sat on the balcony. The "tattoo" or "taps" were sounded, a stanza of Old Hundred—

"Be Thou, O God exalted high,"

was sung and selections from the Nineteenth Psalm were read by Dr. Hale: "A thousand years in Thy sight are but as yesterday when it is past, and as a watch in the night......So teach us to number our days that we may apply our hearts unto wisdom." Sewall's hymn, composed two centuries previously, the second line reads:

"Tame Thou the rigor of our clime,"

was sung and the trumpeters then blew loud notes when silence followed. The bell on Kings Chapel sounding slow, with bells and whistles in all parts of the city, solemnly told the multitude that the

Old Century

had gone.

On Beacon Hill the large crowd—with Governor

Crane—bowing their heads, repeated the Lord's Prayer and sang "America." Dr. Hale pronounced the closing words, "God bless our City, our State and Our Country." The trumpets sounding the *Reveille* closed the exercises. Dr. Hale said, "I do not think they thought of it as a religious service when they came, but they all did when they went away." The scene was most impressive.

The Common has lost much that was picturesque in the last century.

Love in a Cloud,—by Mr. Bates, speaks of the lovers Jack Neligage and Alice Endicott who, when little children, played on the path of the Public Garden. "The smart nursery maids whose occupation it was to convey their charges thither and keep them out of the fountains, between whiles exchanging gossip about the parents of the babies, had begun the talk. The opinions of fashionable society are generally first found by servants, and then served up with a garnish of fancifully distorted facts for the edification of their mistresses; and in due time the loves of the Public Garden, reported and decorated by the nursery maids, serve as topics for afternoon calls. Master Jack was known to be in love with Miss Alice before either of them could have written the word, and in this case the passion had been so lasting that it excited remark not only for itself but as an extraordinary case of unusual constancy."

1901 JANUARY 14.

A Northern Strike, the first in eight years, was seen in the Public Garden. They usually frequent the fens.

MAY 1.

A small flock of Yellow Palm Warblers came to the Common. They sang freely.

Oliver Wendell Holmes, says, in Over the Tea Cups —"Ever since I had a ten cent look at the transit of Venus.....through the telescope in the Mall, the earth has been wholly different to me from what it used to be."

The Sentimentalists,—by Piers, alludes to the walks of Virginia Kent who passed many hours in the Public Garden where she sat on a bench, near the gate, at Commonwealth Avenue, "to watch the gardeners who were taking the stocks out of a flower bed and laying them in a wheelbarrow, then moulding and smoothing the earth.....She contrasted these good workmen with the men sitting about on benches reading newspapers; and wondered what occupation they could have; it seemed to her a witless sort of life. It did not occur to her that most of them were reading the newspapers in search of occupation......From the Pond, nearby, came the frequent tapping of a gong as the swan-boats, with gay awnings, made their leisurely circuits and discharged the tourists."

The novel—Truth Dexter—by Mrs. Mary McNeil, tells of Craighead who, entering the Public Garden, from Arlington Street, proceeds to the house of Mrs. Adams on Beacon Street, "when the flower beds were brilliant with crocuses, tulips, and hyacinths. The smell of the upturned earth was pungent with life. In a single night Spring's bridal tunic had by fairy looms been woven."

1902

MARCH 13.

The Slate-colored Junco came into the Public Garden. They have also been seen on the Common.

APRIL 23.

A Rusty Blackbird was seen on the Common.

APRIL 23.

The Swamp Sparrow was seen, for the only time, on the Common. They have appeared in the Public Garden, but never to stay more than a day, as there are no damp grounds.

MAY 7.

The Water Thrush made its appearance in the Public Garden. They prefer the vicinity of the Pond rather than the trees.

MAY.

A pair of Bluebirds, apparently intending to nest near Park Square, were seen on the Common.

1903

MARCH 6.

The Song Sparrow came into the Public Garden before the snow had disappeared or the ice floated, broken, in the Ponds. They also appear on the Common their notes resembling those of the Purple Finch.

APRIL 5.

A Pine Warbler was seen in the trees of the small island in the Public Garden.

APRIL 23.

The Ruby-crowned Kinglet first came to the Public

Garden. Their sweet song is heard both in the spring and the Autumn.

APRIL.

The Phoebe was seen on the Common and Public Garden. They were always silent.

MAY 20.

A Night Heron was seen, about the Pond, in the Public Garden at an early hour in the morning.

1904 APRIL 7.

A White-breasted Nuthatch was seen among the trees, on Monument Hill, on the Common.

OCTOBER 17.

The call notes of the Palm Warbler were heard, on the grass, in the Public Garden.

OCTOBER 19.

A Java Sparrow was seen, on the slope of Monument Hill, on the Common.

OCTOBER 22.

The notes of a Blue-Gray Gnatcatcher were heard on the northerly side of the Public Garden.

The Field Sparrow was not seen in the Public Garden.

Only one Warbling Vireo had been seen, in the Public Garden, in three years.

1905 MARCH 19.

A Hairy Woodpecker made a long stay in the Public Garden. This was a second spring visit.

April 24.

A broad winged Hawk was seen perched in an elm beside the Frog Pond on the Common.

April 25.

The earliest visit of the Towhee, or Chewink, to the Public Garden. They have never been seen on the Common.

May 3.

A Solitary Sand Piper came into the Public Garden and lit on a stone near the Pond.

May 7.

Two Yellow-throated Vireos were seen in the Public Garden.

May 12.

The Canadian Warbler was first seen in the Public Garden. They are distinguished by a black necklace on a yellow breast.

May 15.

Wilson's Warbler first appeared in the Public Garden They frequent the trees about the Pond.

May 16.

A Bank Swallow was seen, for the second time, flying over the Pond in the Public Garden.

May 25.

A Myrtle Warbler was seen in the Public Garden. They have occasionally appeared on the Common.

May 26.

Thirty Cedar Waxwings—the largest flock—were seen in the Public Garden.

May 27.

The largest number of Black Poll Warblers were seen, among the willows, in the Public Garden. They always appear in the spring.

MAY.

A beautiful Rose-breasted Grosbeak sweetly sang perched on the bough of an elm on the Common, which extended well out on Beacon Street, his notes breaking the quiet of the neighborhood where the residents still slept at an early morning hour.

1906 MARCH 1.

Henry James says, in an article, entitled "Boston," published in the *Fortnightly Review*,—"It was on two or three such loitering occasions, wondering and invoking pauses that had a little vaguely and helplessly perhaps, the changed crest of Beacon Hill for their field—it was at certain of these moments of changed, or rather chilled, contemplation that I felt my small cluster of early associations shrivel to a scarce discernible point. I recall a Sunday afternoon in particular when I hung about the now vaster platform of the State House for a near view of the military monuments erected there, the statues of Generals Hooker and Devens, and for the charm at once, and the pang of feeling the whole backward vista, with all its features, fall from that eminence into grey perspective. The top of Beacon Hill quite rakes, with but a slightly shifting range, the old more definite Boston......

"Let me at all events say for the Park Street Church, while I am still on my hilltop, that the edifice persistently 'holds the note,' as yet, the note of the old felicity, and remains, by so doing, a precious public servant."

APRIL 3.

The Purple Finch was first seen in the Public Garden.

APRIL 30.

A Cat bird first came into the Public Garden. They are usually silent.

MAY 13.

A House Wren was seen on the beds and shrubs in the Public Garden. Their visits are very infrequent.

MAY 23.

The song of a Northern Flicker was heard on the roof of the Sears residence on Arlington Street. They frequently flew to and fro to the Common.

JUNE 16.

A Bob White flew, near the Everett Statue, in the Public Garden.

OCTOBER 26.

Six brown Creepers were in the large trees in the Public Garden. They come regularly in October.

OCTOBER.

There was an unusual number of Red-breasted Nuthatches in the Public Garden.

DECEMBER.

Blackwoods Magazine, an article by Charles Whibley, says:—"The constant mark of Boston is a demure gaiety. An air of quiet festivity encompasses the streets. The houses are elegant, but sternly ordered... The Mall in Beacon Street, if it is the pride, is also characteristic of Boston. For Boston is a city of parks and trees. The famous Common, as those might remember who believe that America sprang into being in a night, has been sacred for nearly three hundred years. Since 1640 it has been the centre of Boston. It has witnessed the tragedies and comedies of an eventful history. . . . .And it is impossible to forget, as you walk its ample spaces, the many old associations which it brings with it from the past."

The Wood Thrush was first seen in the Public Garden.

1907 FEBRUARY 12.

The Redpool, with its characteristic call, was first seen in the Public Garden.

MARCH 23.

A young Pine Grosbeak was seen, for a few minutes, in the Public Garden, early in the morning.

MARCH 26.

The Red Winged Blackbird first came into the Public Garden.

APRIL 10.

Two hundred and fifty Fox Sparrows were seen feeding on the refuse at the bottom of the Pond, where the water had been drawn off, in the Public Garden.

APRIL 22.

Four Vesper Sparrows were seen on the west end of Monument Hill. They were also on the level of the Parade Ground on the Common.

MAY 1.

The Chipping Sparrows showed a preference for the Common and were seen on the slope of the hill.

MAY 10.

Wilson's Thrush was first seen on the Common. Their song is especially loud on a damp day when it has been heard above the din of the city.

May 14.

The first Bobolink was seen flying over the tulip beds in the centre path in the Public Garden.

May 14.

Two Yellow Warblers sang in the Public Garden.

May 18.

A Night Heron flew into the Public Garden at an early hour in the morning. The weather was cloudy.

May 19.

The notes of the cuckoo were heard in the Public Garden. The only time.

May 20.

Five King birds were seen in a tree, in the Public Garden.

May 22.

Ten Magnolia Warblers were in the Public Garden. They usually sing.

May 23.

A Solitary Sand piper flew, near the Pond, in the Public Garden.

May 30.

The Cliff Swallow came, for the second (record) time, into the Public Garden. They come, skimming over the Pond, on cloudy or misty days.

May.

An American Redstart was heard singing in the Public Garden. It remained eight, or ten days.

October 19.

A flock of twenty-one American Pipits were seen flying over the Public Garden, calling as they passed.

October 22.

Eight Canada Geese were seen, flying southward over the Public Garden.

The Spotted Sand piper was seen three times, in the Public Garden, this year.

The Tree Swallow was seen flying back and fourth, across the Pond, in the Public Garden. They come in May.

The Blue-headed Vires was seen, the fourth time, in the Public Garden and remained for a day. They never sang.

Twice the usual number of Black and White Warblers came into the Public Garden remaining three, or four days, the same season.

The greatest number of Brown Thrushes were perched, in the top of a tree, in the Public Garden.

1908 March 20.

Five King birds were seen in a tree in the Public Garden.

March 20.

A Downy Woodpecker made another visit, sounding his rattle call, in the Public Garden. They were also seen on the Common.

March 27.

The Tree Sparrow was seen bathing in the Pond in the Public Garden.

March 31.

The Savanna Sparrows appeared on the Common and in the Public Garden. Their visits were frequent.

April 10.

American Goldfinches were first seen in the Public Garden. It was among their first appearances.

April 28.

A Golden Crowned Kinglet was seen in the elms of the Beacon Street Mall.

May 1.

The Chipping Sparrows showed a preference for the Common and were seen on the slope of the hill.

May 6.

A Hermit Thrush nested on grounds at the corner of Beacon and Arlington Streets. They are very abundant in the Public Garden.

May 12.

A Siskin was seen in the Public Garden. They were quite rare.

May 12.

Five White Crowned Sparrows, in song, were on the Common.

May 12.

About fifty, the largest number of White-throated Sparrows were counted on the Common and in the Public Garden.

May 12.

A large number of Nashville Warblers came to the Common.

May 12.

Two Parula Warblers were on the Common. They abounded in song.

May 12.

The song of the Black-throated Blue Warbler was heard on the Common.

May 12.

Two Chestnut-sided Warblers were seen on the Common.

May 12.

Two Maryland Yellow Throats were seen on the Common.

May 12.

A Black-throated Green Warbler was singing on the Common.

May 13.

The first Robin of the season appeared on the Common. They are among the first to appear in the spring.

May 16.

A Cape May Warbler came for the third time, into the Public Garden. Leaving the Garden it flew out over the buildings on Boylston Street.

May 18.

An Olive Backed Thrush was seen, near the statue, in the Public Garden. Their song resounds.

May 22.

A Bay-breasted Warbler, with fifteen other warblers, were seen in the Public Garden.

May 24.

A Night-hawk was heard over Beacon Hill in the evening.

May 24.

A Humming Bird visited the Public Garden.

May 24.

The Yellow Bellied Flycatcher visited the Public Garden. They were silent.

May 24.

A Tennessee Warbler was seen near the Everett statue in the Public Garden.

May 26.

Thirty Chimney Swifts were seen flying over the Public Garden.

May 27.

A European Goldfinch was seen picking on the grass near the Pond in the Public Garden.

May 30.

A black billed Cuckoo was seen on the bough of a large willow at the northwest corner of the Public Garden.

June.

A Blue Jay was heard in the Public Garden.

July 3.

A Red-eyed Vireo was heard on the Charles Street side of the Public Garden. Their visits are very rare.

September.

Mr. George F. Parkman, a wealthy citizen of Boston, whose residence commanded a fine view of the Common, died leaving a large fortune and bequeathing a fund of over five millions whose income was "to be applied to the maintenance and improvement of the Common and the Parks now existing." The document also reads: "to the City of Boston in the hope and expectation that the Boston Common shall never be diverted from its present use as a public park for the benefit and enjoyment of its citizens."

October 9.

A European Blackbird was seen in a Norway maple, and ten days later, on the limb of an English hawthorn. It was again seen on the beach of the Garden at the head of Marlborough Street.

October 17.

A Connecticut Warbler was seen in a rose bed, near Arlington Street, in the Public Garden.

October.

Two Sapsuckers made a short visit to the Public Garden. They did not stay as long as the Woodpecker.

November 5.

Two White-winged Crossbills flew over the Public Garden towards the Cone trees in the suburbs.

November.

The Chicadee is often seen in the Public Garden.

December 26.

An American Crow was perched in the Public Garden and another was on the Common. Two crows were once seen in a nest on Beacon Street near the Somerset Club and a nestling once fell to the ground and was taken into the Puritan Club on Spencer Street.

December 30.

A small Screech Owl was seen on the bough of a linden tree, near Joy Street, on the Common, and, as night came, it made two short flights toward the Frog Pond and the Union Club House.

The nest of a Baltimore Oriole was seen on the top bough of a willow, near the boat landing, on the Beacon Street Mall.

Some Bronzed Grackles flew over the Common.

The first Cow-bird was seen on the Common and Public Garden.

1909

William Winter, in Old Friends, in the chapter entitled "Old Bohemian Days" says, "The Boston of today presents a strong contrast with the Boston of fifty or sixty years ago. Now it is an Irish Roman Catholic city. Then it was an American Puritan city. Now it is spacious and splendid. Then it was comparatively small and staid. Now it is pervaded with commotion and the attendant racket. Then it was all tranquility. Now it does not hold undisputed and undisputable pre-eminence in literature and journalism. Then it was—and was rightly called,—the Athens of America. In those days I was familiar with every part of it. As a boy I dwelt and sported on old Fort Hill, since reduced to a plain, and made my playground all along the waterside, from Constitution Wharf to Charlestown Bridge. The Common, the Back Bay; the dry docks, the India Wharf warehouses, of which the doors often stood open, liberating delicious, alluring odors of cinnamon and cedar; the T Wharf with its story of Revolutionary times; the granite Custom House, then new, and seeming wonderful; the Quincy Market, then considered a marvel of architecture,—all those things, and many more, were known to me. Many a time did I gaze, awe-stricken at the haunted mansion, deserted and silent, frowning behind its huge walls, in High Street, called and known as 'Harris's Folly.' Many a time did I rove through Theatre Alley and look with juvenile curiosity on the theatre in Federal Street,—little dreaming that the stage was to be a principal theme of my thoughts and writings throughout a long laborious life. From the top of Fort Hill there was, in the vicinity of Hamilton Street, a mysterious winding stairway of stone, down which the adventurous truant could make his way to the precincts of the docks, where much of my boyhood was spent, in consort with other vagrant lads; and many a happy hour did I pass there, sometimes practically investigating newly landed cargoes of sugar; sometimes reclining on the sun-warmed planks of the silent piers and dreaming over the prospect of the moving ship and the distant islands of Boston harbor."

1910

"A Bird's-eye View of Boston in 1850" is in the Boston Public Library.

A "picture of the Hancock House," presented by John Hancock to Samuel Adams to be used as a fire board, is in the possesison of the Misses Storer of Cambridge.

Paul Revere's engraving of the "Liberty Pyramid," erected on the Common, on the day of the celebration of the Repeal of the Stamp Act, May 19, 1766, and burned on that night, is in the Boston Athenaeum.

A "Prospective View of part of the Common," from a water color drawing by Christian Renwick, 1768, is now in the possession of the Concord Antiquarian Society. It shows the camp of the 29th Regiment, field pieces, tents, etc., and was "taken from the grove" in the Common, October, 1768.

A "Staffordshire Platter," beautifully painted with "Cows on the Common," is in the collection of E. R. Warren, Brookline.

"Tremont Street Looking North," from a water color drawing thought to have been painted by a daughter of General Knox, about 1800," is in the Boston Public Library.

"The Common and Beacon Street, 1804-1811" from a water color drawing, is in the Boston Public Library.

A picture of "Tremont Street Mall, showing Colonnade Row" that once appeared on a sheet of music is in the collection of the late Dr. J. F. Ayer.

A "View of the Back Bay, Charles Street and the Common, Boston,"—from a sketch taken from a balcony of 61 Beacon Street, in 1823, is in the Boston Athenaeum.

"Boston Common, 1830," from a water color painted by George Harvey, is in the possession of the Bostonian Society.

"The Pavillion," erected for the Whig celebration on the Common, Fourth of July, 1834, and reproduced by Pendleton, Boston, is in the Boston Public Library.

"Encampment of the Boston Rifle Rangers on the Boston Common," lithographed and published by Henry Prentice in 1842, and which first appeared on a sheet of music, is in the Boston Public Library.

A "View of the Grand Masschusetts Washington Convention" held on the Common, May 30, 1844, taken from a lithograph published by F. Gleason, Boston, is in the Boston Public Library.

"Tremont Street in 1843," drawn on stone by W. Sharp from an original by P. Harry, is in the Boston Public Library.

A photograph of the "Gates of the Boston Common at Park Square," is in the possession of the Boston Athenaeum.

1911 April 17.

A fire broke out on the ground floor of the State House endangering the entire building. The blaze started in a restaurant and was discovered by a pedestrian early in the morning. The flames were confined by the firemen to the restaurant, though some damage was done by the smoke and water.

May 15.

The New York Times says, "Boston (14) An Ordinance was submitted by the Mayor to the City Council consolidating the present Park, Public Grounds, Bath and Music Departments into the Park and Recreation Department......A baseball league is in process of formation. There will also be swimming competition, with provisions for girls as well as boys.....The Ordinance covers the city parks, public grounds, beaches, baths, playgrounds, indoor and outdoor gymnasiums, athletic fields, summer band concerts, winter indoor concerts, etc." The Common figures prominently.

Conclusion.

The Common was bought for one hundred and fifty dollars in 1634. It now has an endowment of five millions. Its future is assured.

The sunsets, and tinted skies, seen from the Common, are ever one of the features.

Other Extracts From Fiction

MY SOUTHERN FRIENDS

by

EDMUND KIRKE WHITE, 1863.

"Long weeks went by, but no answer came; and again she wrote him.

"One day, not long after sending this last letter, as she was crossing the Common to her attic in Charles Street, she met him. He was alone, and saw her, but attempted to pass her without recognition. She stood squarely in his way, and told him she *would* be heard. He admitted having received her letters, but said he could do nothing for her." pp. 32.

"After a time she rose and left the house. As she walked down Beacon Street, the sun was sinking in the west, and its red glow mounted midway up the heavens. As she looked at it, the sky seemed one great molten sea, its hot, livid waves surging all around her. She thought it came nearer; that it set on fire the green Common and the great houses, and shot fierce, hot flames through her brain and into her very soul. For a moment she was paralyzed, and sunk to the ground; then, springing to her feet, she flew to her child. She bounded down the long hill, and up the steep stairways, and burst into the room of the good woman who was tending him, shouting: 'Fire! fire! The world is on fire!'

"She caught him up, and darted away. She flew down Charles Street, across the Common, and through the crowded thoroughfares, till she reached India Wharf, all the while muttering, 'Water, water!'—water, to quench the fire in her blood, in her brain, in her very soul.

"She paused on the pier, and gazed for a moment at the dark, slimy flood; then she plunged down, down, where all is forgetfulness!" pp. 33.

A Politician's Daughter, by Myra Sawyer Hamlin, 1886. "—Miss Harcourt had always breathed and had her own being. Aside from the fact that she would be unacceptable to the Beacon Street set, as the daughter of a politician, would not the Beacon Street set be tiresome to her, with its afternoon teas, where the legends of old families were endlessly served up in ancestral tea-cups, and the virtues of the old bitter against the disabilities of the new? They were very respectable but very slow, those afternoon teas." pp. 68.

Roses of Shadow, a Novel, by T. R. Sullivan, 1885. —"The word dinner is a reminder that its hour was a merry one at the old 'Aegean.' Men dropped in between five and seven to dine, two or three together, in a large room on the second floor overflowing an irregular enclosure behind the house; the servants called this patch of ground 'the garden,' but there flourished in it only dusty grass and vines with a restless dwarf of a fountain, that kept a gilt ball bobbing up and down its tiny jet all the summer time. After dinner, coffee and segars were to be had in the library or, weather permitting, on the stone balcony fronting the street and the double row of great English elms in the mall that bounds the Common. What sunsets those were to be lazily admired or ignored according to the digestive mood of the moment! The new club house turns its back upon them." pp. 2.

Miss Brooks. A Story, by Eliza Orne White, 1890.

"It was a delicious afternoon. The maples on the Common were nearly in full leaf while the later elms were enveloped in a delicate green mist. An east wind, softened by the distance which it had traveled since leaving the sea, had gathered something of the fragrance of the apple-blossoms in the Brookses garden. It expressed to the sense of smell what the faint colors showed to the eye, while the song of robins and blue birds completed the impression to the ear. Every sense was penetrated with the beauty of the spring." pp. 31.

The Chippendales. By Robert Grant, 1909.

"On his way home from the office on the previous afternoon he had made a detour through the so-called Back Bay. He had walked down the sunny slope of Beacon Hill from the State House, where the houses are only on one side, past the Common and along the sidewalk which skirts the Public Garden." pp. 48.

A Boston Girl. A story of Boston, Bar Harbor and Paris, 1886.

"Probably the first out-of-door objects my infant eyes rested on were the magnificent elms across the street, in the grand old Park which bears the modest name of

Boston Common. My earliest travels probably were along these shady paths around the Frog Pond, down across Charles Street, and through the Public Gardens —in a baby carriage." pp. 9 and 10.

A Boston Girl's Ambition. By Virginia F. Townsend, 1887.

"They found minutes to spare for the Public Garden. They saw the tulips in all their glory; a blaze of color that rivalled the sunsets; they lingered by the Pond, or among the brown paths, cooled with dews, and flecked with shadows." pp. 143.

Autocrat of the Breakfast Table, by Oliver Wendell Holmes, 1891.

"I glide around the Back Bay, down the stream, up the Charles to Cambridge and Watertown, up the Mystic, round the wharves in the wake of steamboats, which leave a swell after them delightful to rock upon; I linger under the bridges. Then back to my moorings at the foot of the Common." pp. 164-5.

The Philistines, by Arlo Bates, 1889.

—"While Helen and Herman were walking across the Common to find her, Ninitta was lying amid a heap of gorgeous stuffs and cushions in Fenton's studio, while he painted and talked after his fashion." pp. 71.

Pirate Gold, by F. J. Stimson (J. S. Dale), 1896.

"The next morning, old Mr. James Bowdoin got up even earlier than usual, with an undefined sense of pleasure, as was his wont, he walked across the street to sit half an hour before breakfast in the Common. The old crossing-sweeper was already there, to receive his penny, and the orange woman expectant, sold her apex orange to him for a silver thri' penny bit as his before-breakfast—" pp. 125.

The Bostonians. A Novel, by Henry James, 1886.

—"Basil Ransom, meanwhile, put the question to Mrs Luna—for Mrs. Luna when they reached Beacon Street, would not hear of his leaving her to go her way alone, would not in the least admit his plea that he had only an hour or two more in Boston." pp. 96.

—"There were nights of deep snow-fall when Charles Street was white and muffled and the door-bell foredoomed to silence which seemed little islands of lamplight, of enlarged and intensified vision." pp. 175.

The Rebels, or Boston before the Revolution, by the author of "Hobomok," 1850.

"In the October following, the regiment with several ships of war, arrived in Boston harbor, and drew up as if to blockade the town. In a few days, the barracks at the Castle, the Town House, and Faneuil Hall, were filled; and a long line of tents, here and there surmounted by the red cross standard, stretched across our beautiful Common. Wherever the eye turned, it rested on British uniforms;—wherever the bright sun glanced, it was reflected by British steel." pp. 226.

Lionel Lincoln, by J. Fenimore Cooper.

"Lionel had walked from the dwelling of Mrs. Lechmere to the foot of Beacon Hill, and had even toiled up some part of the steep ascent—continued to ascend until he gained the summit of the eminence. There arose from the town itself a distant buzzing, like the hum of suppressed agitation, and lights were seen to glide along the streets, or flit across the windows, in a manner which denoted that a knowledge of the expedition had become general within the dwellings. Lionel turned his head towards the Common, and listened long and anxiously, but in vain, to detect a single sound that could betray any unusual stir among the soldiery. Towards the interior, the darkness of night had fallen heavily, dimming the amphitheatre of hills that encircled the place, and enshrouding the vales and lowlands between them and the water with an impenetrable veil of gloom." pp. 104.

The Fate of Mansfield Humphreys, by Richard Grant White, 1884.

"But Margaret's great delight was the Common. To this she led Humphrey's step whenever they went out together; into this she wandered alone sometimes when he was from her. 'This,' she said, 'is something like a park; although indeed it's not a very large sort of place. But one feels at rest and at home in it. And what beautiful trees!'" pp. 254.

Twice Told Tales, by Nathaniel Hawthorne.

"'Peace, silly child,' cried he, at last more harshly than he had ever before addressed the gentle Alice. 'The rebuke of a king is more to be dreaded than the clamor of a wild, misguided multitude. Captain Lincoln, it is decided. The fortress of Castle William must be occupied by the royal troops. The two remaining regiments shall be billeted in the town, or encamped upon the Common.'" Vol. 2, pp. 298.

A Little Upstart, a Novel, by William H. Rideing, 1885.

"One of the charms of the Common is that it is in the very heart of the city; it is as central as the Bois de Boulogne would be if it were in the site of the Place de l'Opéra, or as St. James Park if that enclosure had its centre on the site of St. Paul's Cathedral; and while on one side Gerald could see the never-ending, jingling, jostling traffic of Tremont Street, he was faced on three others by compact masses of architecture of a uniform luxuriousness infrequent in American cities. Above the nearly level surface of the roofs shot a group of spires, towers and campaniles, some slender and pointed, others square and open, with glimpses of sky and cloud visible through their arches; and when the sun was dropping behind the hills in the west, they stood out in the blaze with Venetian picturesqueness." pp. 102-3.

A Voyage of Discovery, a Novel, of American Society, by Hamilton Aide, 1892.

—"That same day two of their agreeable acquaintances of the previous evening escorted them to the State House, with its gilded dome and fine eighteenth century decorations. They ascended a lofty tower, and gained a comprehensive view of the city, the winding river, and Charlestown, and beyond it the south coast, island sprinkled sea. It was a clear, brilliant day, though intensely cold. The dark boats on the glittering river, the numerous vanes and pinnacles that rose above the snow-bound city and caught the sunlight, the forest of masts in the harbor and silhouettes of wide-armed elms upon the Common, the frozen lake on which hundreds were skating and sliding merrily, and over all a span of wind-swept sky, almost Florentine in its hard, blue depth, startled the English travellers with unexpected beauty. 'This is really charming?' cried

Mrs. Trampton, and after such an admission there was nothing more to be said. They visited several book stores and the noble public library. At last, when the sky was growing the color of a tea-rose, against which church tower and steeple uprose in solid purple, they recrossed the park, and Grace and Morduant hastened to dress for the Country Club dinner." pp. 283-4.

An American Politician, a Novel, by F. Marion Crawford, 1885.

"The next day he rose early and 'did' Boston. It did not take him long, he said to himself that half of it was very jolly, and half of it was too utterly beastly for anything. The Common, and the Garden, and Commonwealth Avenue, you know, were rather pretty, and must have cost a deuce of a lot of money in this country; but as for the State House, and Paul Revere's Church, and the Old South, and the city generally, why, it was simply disgusting, all that, you know, and in the afternoon we went to see Sybil Brandon, and began talking about what he had seen." pp. 161.

—"The trees on the Common are thick and heavy with foliage, the Public Garden is a carpet of bright flowers, and on the walls of Beacon Street the great creepers have burst into blossom and are stretching long shoots over the brown stone and the iron balconies. There is a smell of violets and flowers in the warm air, and down on the little pond the swan-shaped boats are paddling about with their cargoes of merry children and calico nursery-maids, while the Irish boys look on from the banks and throw pebbles when the policemen are not looking, wishing they had the spare coin necessary to embark for a ten minute's voyage on the mimic sea." pp. 281.

A Child of the Century. By John T. Wheelwright, 1887.

—"Sewall...... his whole life had been spent on that part of the earth's surface which is contained in a circle with a radius of five miles, and with the tarnished gilt dome of the State House as a centre......The trees on the Common waved their limbs in welcome to him, like old friends, when he passed along the mall. On Beacon Hill, the once proud eminence, now being deserted by the fashionable and invaded by boarding-house keepers stands his grandfather's pleasant old fashioned house, in which he passed his boyhood...... Over beyond the Common, the 'Coasting,' football, and battle ground of his boyhood, was the school house where he laid the foundations of that ripe culture for which he was pre-eminent even in Boston." pp. 3-4.

"It was not unnatural, then, that his blood tingled through his body when he sniffed the salt breeze flowing over the Back Bay as he took his regular afternoon constitutional between the hours of 4.30 and 5.30 p. m." pp. 6.

Rowena in Boston, a Novel, by Maria Louise Pool, 1892.

—"Sometimes, when she went out for a bit of butter or some rolls, she would walk up to a brighter part of the city and stroll across the Common, thinking it was a very poor make-believe of the country." pp. 80.

—"Instead of going to her room Rowena wandered across the Common and out towards the Public Gardens. She was senselessly irritated and despondent. Her art was drudgery." pp. 109.

—"Vanessa must have been thoroughly in earnest in

what she had said to him on the Common of her interest in that girl." pp. 320-1.

—"The long June twilight was gone, and a dusk, odorous even here in the city, was coming among the trees on the Common when Rowena rose to go back to her shabby little room and to the Yorkshire. This latter individual had been trying to beguile his ennui by a complete destruction of a pin-cushion which George Warner had made and presented to the friend who had gone to Boston to learn to paint." pp. 324.

Wheel of Fire, by Arlo Bates, 1885.

—"She crossed the Common with throbbing temples and a buoyancy of mood which was far too ecstatic to be natural, and which might have made one intimately acquainted with her antecedents tremble a little from fear of the reaction which should follow." pp. 284.

—"She had no reason for surmising that the time had come when he had but to speak to win the consent he so fervently desired; and the pair walked side by side across the Common, as far from understanding each other as if separated by continents." pp. 296.

The Pagans, by the same author, 1884.

—"Going across the Common toward the studio on the sunny morning, when the air was brisk and bracing, the naked trees clearly and delicately defined against the sky, Helen's thoughts went back to her past; to her shy, secluded girlhood, to the years of her married life, and to the way in which she had been living since she and her husband parted. She reflected with a smile, half pity, half contempt, of the proud, reticent girl who had pored over books and drawings in the musty, deserted library at home, almost wondering if she were the same being. She looked from the Joy Street Mall across the hollow which holds the Frog Pond, the most charming view on the Common, yet not even the golden sparkle of the water or the beautiful line of the slope beyond could chase from her mind the picture of the high, dim old room, lined to the ceiling with book shelves, dusty from neglect." pp. 67-8.

—"They crossed the Common, chatting idly, and both conscious that the frankness of their old intercourse was somewhat lacking." pp. 123.

—"She walked briskly through the bracing morning across the Common, her mind full of bright fancies." pp. 213.

—"He went to the round window, for his studio was high up in the building, and removed the Japanese umbrella which served as its screen. He threw himself upon a pile of cushions, regarding darkly the tops of the trees in the old Granary burying ground opposite." pp. 265.

Miss Curtis, a Sketch, by Kate Gannett Wells, 1888.

"Two quaint little figures were walking up Beacon Street with that old fashioned air which belongs to immature responsibility when there is something to be done that is of greater importance to the doer than to any one else. 'Do you suppose, Olive, that we've got to make grateful calls when you are a teacher and I'm in college?'

" 'I rather go without things, Owen, than have to take some things and have to thank people for other things,' was the eager, vexed reply, 'but don't let us talk, I'm 'fraid I shall forget. It is just like learning your part in a play. First it is a 'How do you do,' and 'How do the family do,' and 'How do I do,' and then it is weather; and then it is how old you are, and where you go to school; and next it is general news; and then it is advice; and last it is good-bye,' and the little face looked out of its mass of short brown curls as if it saw in every passer-by a stage prompter, who hissed at her the opening words of each sentence." pp. 9-10.

Captain Nelson—a Romance of Colonial Days, by Samuel Adams Drake, 1879.

"The triple crown of hills which dominated the peninsula rose above a motley collection of houses crowded along the strand or scattered upon the hillsides. Those by the shore indicated the commercial character of the place; those on the hills were the homes of the more wealthy citizens. Seen at a distance, the effect was sufficiently picturesque; the three little mountains had already taken a character agreeing with the needs of the plantation. On the green crest of the highest summit a tall shaft, designed to give timely warning of the approach of evening, was the conspicuous object, far and near. A second eminence, topped by a wind mill, ascended at the peninsula's extreme seaward limit; a third having its foot also washed by the sea, was crowned by a fortress, whose artillery swept the roadstead. The beacon, the windmill, and the fortress were thus the prominent landmarks of the town, and from them the hills of Tri-mountain were long familiarly distinguished." pp. 11.

Penelope's Suitors—by Edwin Lassetter Bymer, 1887.

1639—"No. 1.20 I became acquainted with the family, and rest well content. Here is much more after than at home, for besides that the governor hath divers visitors upon ceremony and business daily, his dwelling is placed upon the chief street where is much passing to and fro. It is a large house, quite plain without, but well-ordered within. Both the governor and madam are most gracious to me, and account themselves kinsfolk, it seemeth with brother Herbert, through his wife. Yesterday, Mr. Deane came civilly and bade me forth for an outing. We walked upon the Centry Field, and thence by the sea-shore to Mr. Blackstone's garden, where he had good prospect of the the sun's setting." pp. 14.

Agnes Surriage, by the same author, 1887.

"The old 'Bunch of Grapes' tavern in Boston was ablaze with light. From the front window it streamed across Kings Street in a broad white ribbon and lit up with a feeble glare the eastern gable of the Town House. Something unusual was astir in the old hostlery. Guests were arriving in chairs and chaises, and the heavy door swinging open from time to time to admit them, showed in vivid relief against the outer blackness the wistful faces of a knot of idlers hanging about the entrance, straining their ears to catch a stray word from the hum of jocund voices within, and sniffing with eager noses the savory odors from the kitchen." pp. 21.

A Great Treason. A Story of the War of Independence, by Mary A. M. Hoppus, 1883.

—"On that same Tuesday evening, Lieutenant Digby happened to be crossing the Common with Lord Percy, whom he had known in England, and who was always very civil to him. Percy was returning to quarters from a conference with the Governor, and had just said to Fred that he might tell him in strict secrecy that a blow would be struck before very long, when they observed a group of men standing under some trees. It was a clear evening, with the moon in her last quarter, just rising." pp. 113.

Suburban Sketches, by W. D. Howells, 1871.

"By Horse-car to Boston." "Thanks to mansard curves and dormer windows of the newer houses, there is a singularly picturesque variety among the roofs that stretch along the bay, and rise one above another on the city's three hills, grouping themselves about the State House, and surmounted by its India-rubber dome, but, after all, does human weakness crave some legendary charm, some grace of uncertain antiquity, in the picturesqueness it sees? I own that the future, to which we are often referred for the 'stuff that dreams are made of,' is more difficult for the fancy than the past, that the airy amplitude of its possibilities is somewhat chilly, and that we naturally long for the snug quarters of old, made warm by many generations of life." pp 108.

The Wolf at the Door. 1877.

—"The gray horses went on, and they reached the Chestnut Hill Reservoir, rolling over the smooth roadway, broken here and there with muddy spots, and there were patches of snow, and some of October's brown leaves lying beneath the bare trees, heaped up here and there or blown across the path. As they turned to come back, they saw a red purple haze sinking over the town, and presently the gilt dome of the State House glittering far away in the midst." pp. 58.

The Scarlet Letter, by Nathaniel Hawthorne.

—"Here to witness the scene which we are describing, sat Governor Bellingham himself, with four sergeants about his chair, bearing halberds as a guard of honor. He wore a dark feather in his hat, a border of embroidery on his cloak, and a black velvet tunic beneath; a gentleman advanced in years, with a hard experience written in his wrinkles. He was not ill-fitted to be the head and representative of a community, which owed its origin and progress, and its present state of development not to the impulses of youth, but to the stern and tempered energies of manhood, and the sombre sagacity of age; accomplishing so much precisely because it imagined and hoped so little. The other eminent characters, by whom the chief ruler was surrounded, were distinguished by a dignity of mien, belonging to a period when the forms of authority were felt to possess the sacredness of Divine institution."

—"Without further adventure, they reached the dwelling of Governor Bellingham. This was a large wooden house, built in a fashion of which there are specimens still extant in the streets of our older towns; now moss-grown, crumbling to decay, and melancholy at heart with the many joyful or sorrowful occurrences remembered or forgotten, that have happened, and passed away, within their dusky chambers. Then, however, there was the freshness of the passing year on its exterior, and the cheerfulness, gleaming forth from the sunny windows, of a human habitation, into which death had never entered. It had, indeed, a very cheery aspect; the walls being overspread with a kind of stucco, in which fragments of broken glass were plentifully intermixed; so that, when the sunshine fell aslantwise over the front of the edifice it glittered and sparkled as if diamonds had been flung against it by the double handful. The brilliancy might have befitted Aladdin's palace, rather than the mansion of a grave old Puritan ruler."

—"In the open air their rapture broke into speech. The street and the market-place absolutely babbled from side to side, with applauses of the minister. His hearers could not rest until they had told one another of what each knew better than he could tell or hear. According to their united testimony, never had man spoken in so wise, so high, and so holy a spirit, as he that spake this day."

The Siege of the Seven Suitors, by Meredith Nicholson, 1910.

—"who wore that slipper and dropped it as it seemed from the clouds, at my feet there in sedate Beacon Street, that most solemn of residential sancturies."

" 'Mr. Ames,' began Miss Hollister instantly, with an assumed severity that her smile belied, 'I cannot recall that my niece Hezekiah ever visited in Beacon Street; yet I dare say that if she had done so and a young man of your pleasing appearance had passed beneath her window, one of her slippers might very easily have become detached from Hezekiah's foot and fallen with a nice calculation directly in front of you.' " pp. 263.

"Hezekiah on the roof was safe for a time. Miss Octavia's gentle rejection of my Beacon Street anecdote and her intimation that Hezekiah had been an unfilled participant in the comedy of the ghost had been disquieting, and in my relief at her abandonment of the search I loitered on downstairs with my hostess."

—" 'And whether that slipper really fell at your feet in Beacon Street or even in the less likely precincts of Rittenhouse Square, or under the windows of the

Spanish Embassy in Washington, I believe that you are my good knight, and that you will see me safely through this singular adventure.' " pp. 274.

Miss Theodora, A West End Story, by Helen Leah Reed, 1898.

"The tourist with his day or two at a downtown hotel, calls Boston a city of narrow streets and ancient graveyards; the dweller in one of the newer avenues is enthusiastic about the modern architecture and regular streets of the Back Bay region. Yet neither of these knows the real Boston, the old West End, with its quaint tree-lined streets sloping from the top of Beacon Hill toward the river.

"Near the close of any bright afternoon, walk from the State House down the hill, pause halfway, and glancing back note the perfect Gothic arch formed by the trees that line both sides of Mount Vernon Street. Admire those old houses which have taken on the rich, deep tones that age so kindly imparts to brick. Then look across the river to the sun just setting behind the Brookline Hills,—and admit that even in a crowded city we may catch glimpses of the picturesque." pp. 1-2.

—"It's shameful that the Somersets should think so little of themselves as to move from Chestnut to Beacon Street; and their new house isn't even opposite the Public Garden." pp. 16.

—"How disturbed she had been walking up Beacon Street one day, to see workmen tearing down one of the most dignified of the old purple windowed houses, once the home of intimate friends of hers, to make way for an uglier if more ornate structure! What an intrusion she felt the car tracks to be which run through Charles

Street across Beacon Street, continuing through South and the West ends of the city?

"Miss Theodosia's Boston was not so large but that it could be traversed by any healthy person on foot,—" pp. 151-2.

April Hopes, by W. D. Howells, 1888.

" 'You can sit in the Garden, and wait for the next car.' "

" 'No, I would rather go back to the Art Museum, and make a fresh start.' "

" 'To the Art Museum?' she murmured tenderly."

" 'Yes. Wouldn't you like to see it again?' "

" 'Again? I should like to pass my whole life in it.' " pp. 210.

"He walked back to Charles Street by the Garden path, keeping abreast of her, and not losing sight of her for a moment, except when the bulk of a string team watering at the trough beside the pavement intervened." pp. 216.

Memories of a Millionaire, by Lucia True Ames, 1889.

"Boston, Jan. 6, 26, Louisburg Square.

Jessie Dear.—I have been sitting for the last half-hour in the broad cushioned window-seat of my cozy attic room looking far out over the mass of chimney-tops to the towers and spires beyond the hills and the Public Garden.

"I love to sit here quietly on Sunday afternoon, and when the sunset comes I throw aside my books and watch the shifting brilliant colors turning the blue Charles into a sheet of glimmering gold and dying with rosy hues the snowy slopes of Corey Hill beyond.

"Have you been away so long as to have forgotten those dear old sights? And do you recall that on this western slope of Beacon Hill from which I write to you lived the hermit Blackstone of Shawmut, before Winthrop or any Puritan had thought of settling Boston town? I like old places. I like to be on the oldest spot in this old, historic town, as you may easily imagine remembering all my antiquarian enthusiasm when we were at school." pp. 19-20.

Man Proposes. A Novel, 1880.

—" 'Really Mr. Prescott, it is time for us to leave town. The summer is coming in earnest, and we can't stay longer.' 'June, my dear, is the first month in the year in Boston. Just think what glorious resort the Common would be at this season if it were only in Newport.' Here the cheroot was raised to an angle of forty-five degrees, bearing east by south towards the lady. 'But it isn't in Newport; and it might as well be built over, for all the good it does us. *We* can't walk there.'

" 'And why not, my dear?'

" 'Why do you know the walks are always filled with country cousins, and strollers that have nothing to do, and people that go holding each others hands; and the seats are occupied with queer, staring couples.' There was a shrug or shiver of disgust.

" 'Part of the entertainment, my dear, these strange folks make the walks a study. And they can't spoil all the fresh air, nor use all the green shade, nor monopolize the blue sky.'

" 'No, but refined people like privacy. These low cads and shop-girls would make the finest park vulgar. No lady in society is even seen on the Common, except in crossing to St. Paul's on Sunday morning. So much the worse for them.'" pp. 19-20.

—"It was not for such a man, when once aroused, to content himself with timid monosyllables in the presence of his beloved. He had broken away from the office of Prescott & Co., by some resistless impulse, and strode out for a walk. As he neared the Common, the elms seemed to wave him a welcome, and the long brown malls opened invitingly. Cool airs played with his hair as he raised his hat under the shade; and the peace of the blue heaven came through the open work of leaves." pp. 46-7.

A Country Doctor, by Sarah Orne Jewett, 1884.

"Nan looked on with sympathetic eyes, or watched the squirrels in the trees of the quiet Granary Burying Ground, which seemed to her like a bit of country which the noisy city had caught and imprisoned." pp. 151.

A Fountain Sealed, by Anne Douglas Sedgwick, 1908.

"Jack's aunt lived in a peaceful house on the hill, and the windows of Jack's large flat, nearby, looked over the Common, the Gardens, the Charles River, a cheerful bird's-eye view of the tranquil city, breathed upon now by the first, faint green of spring." pp. 140.

THE BEACON.

Full fourscore years have passed me by;
Chair-bound and feeble, at my window, I
Look out upon the aging world,
Half sad, half glad, to know the end so nigh.

Below me, many housetops hide
The secrets of a thousand lives inside—
Protect their joys, loves, griefs, and sins.
Ah! I have known all these—and more beside!

I've drunk of life in many lands
Full draughts! No cup withheld, untasted, stands—
Save one, from which we all must drink,
And this, when emptied, drops from lifeless hands.

Sundown's trailed by a dying rose . . .
But wind-bent trees a golden cross disclose,
Spire high! So, in my dark'ning room,
Alone, I wait in peace for night's repose.

Louise Von Wetter in the New York Times.

BOSTON.

Oh, say,
Ain't Boston gay
To-day?
Ain't the sacred Codfish grinning
Like a Cheshire cat that's et
A flock of Giant canaries
And wants a few more yet?
Ain't the Golden Dome of the State
House
Got splints bound on it tight
So's not to bust wide open
In spasms of delight?
Ain't the famous Frog Pond bubbling
Like Lethe on the lave,
With all of Boston singing
"A life on the ocean wave"?
Ain't a dog of war at present
A brindled Boston pup?

Ain't pork and beans just booming
And the price still going up?
Oh, say,
Ain't Boston gay
To-day?
She's laid her intellect aside
And counts her brains as nit,
While, Beacon Street and Common folks
Let loose and throw a fit.
Her Mayflower is a hopeless wreck,
Her whirling Hub is still,
Tea parties are forgotten now,
There ain't no Bunker Hill.
Wow,
Do you mind that now?
And why, oh, why,
Are they all knocked into pie?
My scat,
Don't you know that?
Haven't you heard the news from Boston,
How the Red Sox won the game
That crowns the modern Boston
And swats her ancient fame?
The past is nothing to Boston
Now that her pork and beans
Has walloped the Broadway lobster
And swiped Manhattan's jeans.
Oh, say,
Ain't Boston gay
To-day?
And New York? Well,
Maybe it ain't hades
And maybe it is.
Gee whiz!!!

W. J. Lampton, in the New York Times.